英诗经典名家名译

美国现代诗选（下）

英汉对照

赵毅衡 编译

ANTHOLOGY OF
MODERN AMERICAN
POETRY

外语教学与研究出版社
FOREIGN LANGUAGE TEACHING AND RESEARCH PRESS
北京 BEIJING

图书在版编目(CIP)数据

美国现代诗选. 下:英汉对照 / 赵毅衡编译. -- 北京:外语教学与研究出版社,2019.8(2020.10重印)
(英诗经典名家名译)
ISBN 978-7-5213-1156-3

Ⅰ. ①美… Ⅱ. ①赵… Ⅲ. ①英语-汉语-对照读物②诗集-美国-现代 Ⅳ. ①H319.4:Ⅰ

中国版本图书馆 CIP 数据核字 (2019) 第 187940 号

出 版 人　徐建忠
责任编辑　杨雨昕
责任校对　易　璐
封面设计　王　润
出版发行　外语教学与研究出版社
社　　址　北京市西三环北路 19 号（100089）
网　　址　http://www.fltrp.com
印　　刷　三河市北燕印装有限公司
开　　本　889×1194　1/32
印　　张　21
版　　次　2019 年 9 月第 1 版　2020 年 10 月第 2 次印刷
书　　号　ISBN 978-7-5213-1156-3
定　　价　59.00 元（上下册）

购书咨询:（010）88819926　电子邮箱:club@fltrp.com
外研书店:https://waiyants.tmall.com
凡印刷、装订质量问题,请联系我社印制部
联系电话:（010）61207896　电子邮箱:zhijian@fltrp.com
凡侵权、盗版书籍线索,请联系我社法律事务部
举报电话:（010）88817519　电子邮箱:banquan@fltrp.com
物料号:311560001

目录

249 **T. S. 艾略特**
(Thomas Stearns Eliot, 1888–1965)

250 The Love Song of J. Alfred Prufrock　J. 阿尔弗雷德·普鲁弗洛克的情歌

264 Preludes　序曲

266 La Figlia Che Piange　哭泣的姑娘

268 Morning at the Window　窗前晨景

270 Aunt Helen　海伦姑妈

272 The Hippopotamus　河马

276 Whispers of Immortality (Excerpts)　不朽的低语（选段）

278 Sweeney Among the Nightingales　斯威尼在夜莺之间

282 Gerontion　小老头

290 The Waste Land　荒原

346 The Hollow Men　空心人

356 Journey of the Magi　三贤哲的旅程

361 **华莱斯·斯蒂文斯**
(Wallace Stevens, 1879–1955)

362 Domination of Black　黑色的统治

364 The Snow Man　雪中人

366 Valley Candle　山谷中的蜡烛

368 The Emperor of Ice-cream　冰淇淋皇帝

370 Anecdote of the Jar　坛子的轶事

372 Peter Quince at the Clavier　彼得·昆士弹琴

380　Thirteen Ways of Looking at a Blackbird　看黑鸟的十三种方式
386　The Death of a Soldier　士兵之死
388　Dance of the Macabre Mice　恐怖的鼠之舞
390　The Man with the Blue Guitar (Excerpts)　弹蓝色吉他的人（选段）
394　Dry Loaf　干面包
398　Of Modern Poetry　论现代诗歌
400　The Motive for Metaphor　比喻的动机
402　Notes Toward a Supreme Fiction (Excerpts)　最高虚构笔记（选段）

407　**罗宾森·杰弗斯**
　　（Robinson Jeffers, 1887-1962）

408　Divinely Superfluous Beauty　神圣的多余的美
408　To the Stone-cutters　致凿石工
410　Summer Holiday　夏天的假日
412　Gale in April　四月劲风
414　Hurt Hawks　受伤的鹰
420　Hands　手
422　Evening Ebb　晚间退潮
424　New Mexican Mountain　新墨西哥山中
426　Love the Wild Swan　爱野天鹅
428　Shine, Perishing Republic　闪耀吧，正在朽败的共和国
432　Clouds of Evening　晚云
434　Grey Weather　灰蒙蒙的天气
436　Rock and Hawk　岩和鹰
438　Watch the Lights Fade　暮望

441　**E. E. 肯明斯**
　　（Edward Estlin Cummings, 1894-1962）

442　in Just—　正是——

444	Spring is like a perhaps hand 春天像一只或许的手
446	Humanity i love you 人类我爱你
450	since feeling is first 既然感情第一
452	next to of course god america i 当然仅仅次于上帝美国我
454	my sweet old etcetera 我那可爱的如此等等
456	somewhere i have never travelled, gladly beyond 有个地方我从未去过，在经验之外
458	anyone lived in a pretty how town 任何人住在一个多美小城
462	love is more thicker than forget 爱情比忘却厚
464	plato told 柏拉图对他
468	let it go—the 让它走——这
470	when life is quite through with 当生命已经告终
472	when faces called flowers float out of the ground 当称作花朵的面容从大地浮起

475　哈特·克兰
(Hart Crane, 1899–1932)

476	My Grandmother's Love Letters 外婆的情书
478	Black Tambourine 黑手鼓
480	North Labrador 北拉布拉多
482	At Melville's Tomb 在梅尔维尔墓前
484	Island Quarry 岛上采石场
486	The Bridge 桥
490	The Return 归来

493　伊莉诺·怀利
(Elinor Wylie, 1885–1928)

494	Escape 潜逃
496	Pretty Words 可爱的词儿

499 **埃德娜·圣-文森特·米蕾**
(Edna St. Vincent Millay, 1892–1950)

500 God's World 上帝的世界
502 "What Lips My Lips Have Kissed, and Where, and Why" "我的唇吻过谁的唇,在哪里,为什么"
504 The Goose-girl 养鹅姑娘
504 Never May the Fruit Be Plucked 永远别摘果子
506 Wild Swans 野天鹅
508 For Pao-chin, a Boatman on the Yellow Sea 致黄海船夫鲍金
510 Justice Denied in Massachusetts 在马萨诸塞正义被拒绝
514 On Hearing a Symphony of Beethoven 听贝多芬的交响乐
516 For You There Is No Song 悼歌

519 **克劳德·麦开**
(Claude McKay, 1889–1948)

520 Spring in New Hampshire 新罕布什尔之春
520 If We Must Die 哪怕我们必死
522 America 美国
524 Harlem Shadows 哈莱姆的孤影

527 **康梯·喀伦**
(Countee Cullen, 1903–1946)

528 Incident 一桩事情
528 For a Lady I Know 为一个我认识的夫人代书
530 From the Dark Tower 从黑塔上

533 **简·吐默**
(Jean Toomer, 1894–1967)

534 Song of the Son 儿子的歌

536	Harvest Song	收割歌
540	Her Lips Are Copper Wire	她的嘴唇是电线

543　兰斯敦·休斯
(Langston Hughes, 1902–1967)

544	The Negro	黑人
546	The Negro Speaks of Rivers	黑人谈河
548	As I Grew Older	我长大了
552	I, Too	我，也来
554	Brass Spittoons	铜痰盂
558	Song for a Dark Girl	为一个黑姑娘唱的歌
558	Merry-go-round	回转木马
560	Uncle Tom	汤姆叔叔
562	Silhouette	侧影
564	Harlem	哈莱姆
566	Troubled Woman	痛苦的女人
566	Ardella	阿黛拉

569　西奥多·罗斯克
(Theodore Roethke, 1908–1963)

570	Open House	开门的房屋
572	Root Cellar	储球根的地窖
572	Cuttings	插枝
574	Cuttings (Later)	续插枝
576	Night Crow	夜半乌鸦
576	The Far Field (Excerpts)	远方的土地（选段）

581　**兰达尔·贾雷尔**
　　(Randall Jarrell, 1914–1965)

582　Eighth Air Force　第八航空队
584　The Death of the Ball Turret Gunner　旋转炮塔射手之死
584　The Range in the Desert　沙漠靶场
588　Well Water　井水

591　**西尔维娅·普拉斯**
　　(Sylvia Plath, 1932–1963)

592　Man in Black　穿黑衣的人
594　Medallion　徽章
598　Morning Song　晨歌
600　The Applicant　申请人
604　Poppies in October　十月的罂粟花
606　Words　词儿
608　Daddy　爹爹
618　The Couriers　快邮
620　Crossing the Water　渡湖

T. S. 艾略特
(Thomas Stearns Eliot, 1888-1965)

艾略特在现代英美诗坛和文论界居盟主地位足有几十年，他在1948年获诺贝尔文学奖，他的影响深深地渗入现代英美文学，甚至有人说现代美国诗歌只有"艾略特派"与"非艾略特派"之分。

艾略特出身于新英格兰文化望族，家庭塑造了他的宗教信仰和教育背景。他就学于哈佛大学，后在巴黎大学、牛津大学深造。早在1911年他就开始写诗，1915年发表第一首诗《J. 阿尔弗雷德·普鲁弗洛克的情歌》，风格已相当成熟，但直到1922年《荒原》出版，他才一举成名，成为现代英美文学界最重要的诗人之一。这首长诗以似乎互不相关的戏剧性片段和各种引语典故拼合而成，以古代生殖神崇拜作为最基本的象征结构；作者用这种独创的形式表现了一战后人们对资本主义世界的厌倦、失望和对未来的悲观与恐惧。1925年的《空心人》一诗更延续和发展了这种绝望感。因此，他这时期的作品被认为是"迷惘的一代"之先声。

20世纪20年后期起，艾略特的思想日趋保守，1927年，他宣布自己"文学上是古典主义者，政治上是保皇主义，宗教上是英国国教——天主教徒"。他后期的诗，如1930年的《圣灰节》和1943年的《四个四重奏》都表明了他对保守主义的精神追求。

艾略特也写了大量的文学批评论著，他的早期文论是20世纪30年代后期形成的"新批评派"的源头之一。艾略特长期担任《标准》杂志主编，并参与主持著名的"费伯与费伯出版社"(Faber and Faber)，这都对他的文学思想产生极大影响，这种影响到20世纪60年代才渐渐消退。

艾略特还写过现代诗剧，如《大教堂中的谋杀》，相当成功，成为文学史经典。

英美两国的现代文学史都要论述艾略特。本书只选译艾略特加入英国籍之前（含1927年）的作品。

The Love Song of J. Alfred Prufrock

>   S'io credessi che mia risposta fosse
>   A persona che mai tornasse al mondo,
>   Questa fiamma staria senza piu scosse.
>   Ma perciocche giammai di questo fondo
>   Non torno vivo alcun, s'i'odo il vero,
>   Senza tema d'infamia ti rispondo.

Let us go then, you and I,
When the evening is spread out against the sky
Like a patient etherized upon a table;
Let us go, through certain half-deserted streets,
The muttering retreats
Of restless nights in one-night cheap hotels
And sawdust restaurants with oyster-shells:
Streets that follow like a tedious argument
Of insidious intent
To lead you to an overwhelming question…
Oh, do not ask, "What is it?"
Let us go and make our visit.

In the room the women come and go
Talking of Michelangelo.

J. 阿尔弗雷德·普鲁弗洛克的情歌

> 要是我相信我在回答的
> 是个能够回到阳世的人,
> 这火焰就不再抖动。
> 可是,如果我听说的是真情,
> 从来没人活着离开深渊,
> 我回答你,不怕于名有损。[1]

那么,让我们走,你和我,

当暮色背靠着天空伸展,

像被麻醉的病人躺在手术台上;

让我们走,穿过行人稀少的街道,

走过通夜难眠的廉价客店

人声喊喳的僻静角落,

走过满地锯屑与牡蛎壳的饭馆:

街连着街,像冗长的辩论

居心不善

把你引向那难以回答的问题……

哦,别问个所以然,

让我们走,去拜见。

房间里女人来去如梭,

老是在谈米开朗琪罗。

---

[1] 题引诗原为意大利语原文,见但丁《神曲·地狱篇》第 27 章。

The yellow fog that rubs its back upon the window-
    panes,
The yellow smoke that rubs its muzzle on the
    window-panes,
Licked its tongue into the corners of the evening,
Lingered upon the pools that stand in drains,
Let fall upon its back the soot that falls from
    chimneys,
Slipped by the terrace, made a sudden leap,
And seeing that it was a soft October night,
Curled once about the house, and fell asleep.

And indeed there will be time
For the yellow smoke that slides along the street,
Rubbing its back upon the window-panes;
There will be time, there will be time
To prepare a face to meet the faces that you meet;
There will be time to murder and create,
And time for all the works and days of hands
That lift and drop a question on your plate;
Time for you and time for me,
And time yet for a hundred indecisions,
And for a hundred visions and revisions,
Before the taking of a toast and tea.

黄雾在窗子上蹭背,

黄烟在窗子上蹭嘴,

舌头舔着夜晚的四角,

在干涸的水坑上徘徊,

烟囱掉出的煤灰落在它背上,

它从阳台边溜过,突然跳起,

但它看到这是温柔的十月之夜,

又蜷缩在房子周围,沉沉入睡。

确实有个时间[1]

让黄烟沿街滑行

在窗子上蹭背;

有个时间,有个时间,

准备一张脸去面对你会见的脸;

有个时间,用来杀人,用来创造,

让那些举起问题又丢进你盘里的手

去完成工作,结束一天天日子。

有个时间给你,有个时间给我,

有个时间先来一百个犹豫,

先来一百个观察,一百个修正,

然后再去吃茶点。

---

[1] 全诗反复说的"有个时间……",是套用《圣经·传道书》第三章的语句:"每一物都有其季节,天底下每一物都有其时间:有生的时间,死的时间,种的时间,收的时间,杀的时间,活的时间……"

In the room the women come and go
Talking of Michelangelo.

And indeed there will be time
To wonder, "Do I dare?" and, "Do I dare?"
Time to turn back and descend the stair,
With a bald spot in the middle of my hair—
(They will say: "How his hair is growing thin!")
My morning coat, my collar mounting firmly to the chin,
My necktie rich and modest, but asserted by a simple pin—
(They will say: "But how his arms and legs are thin!")
Do I dare
Disturb the universe?
In a minute there is time
For decisions and revisions which a minute will reverse.

For I have known them all already, known them all:
Have known the evenings, mornings, afternoons,
I have measured out my life with coffee spoons;
I know the voices dying with a dying fall
Beneath the music from a farther room.
    So how should I presume?

房间里女人来去如梭,
老是在谈米开朗琪罗。

确实总有个时间,
问一声:"我敢不敢?""我敢不敢?"
总有个时间转身走下楼梯,
头发夹带了一个秃斑——
(人们会说:"他头发越来越稀!")
我的晨礼服,顶住下巴,领子笔挺,
我的领结华丽又文静,只用一个简朴的扣针固定,
(人们会说:"他的手臂和腿可真细!")
我敢不敢
把宇宙扰乱?
一分钟内就必须做出
决定和修正,过一分钟再推翻。

我早就熟悉她们每个人,全都熟悉,
我已经熟悉晚上、下午、早晨,
我已经用咖啡匙量过我的一生;
我熟悉远处房间传来的音乐声里
那渐渐变轻而终于消失的人声,
  可我哪敢冒昧行事?

And I have known the eyes already, known them all—
The eyes that fix you in a formulated phrase,
And when I am formulated, sprawling on a pin,
When I am pinned and wriggling on the wall,
Then how should I begin
To spit out all the butt-ends of my days and ways?
    And how should I presume?

And I have known the arms already, known them
    all—
Arms that are braceleted and white and bare
(But in the lamplight, downed with light brown hair!)
Is it perfume from a dress
That makes me so digress?
Arms that lie along a table, or wrap about a shawl.
    And should I then presume?
    And how should I begin?

    *   *   *   *

Shall I say, I have gone at dusk through narrow streets
And watched the smoke that rises from the pipes
Of lonely men in shirt-sleeves, leaning out of
    windows?...

I should have been a pair of ragged claws
Scuttling across the floors of silent seas.

    *   *   *   *

我早就熟悉这些眼睛,全都熟悉——
它们把你固定在一句程式化的短语中,
当我被程式化,趴在一根针下,
当我被钉在墙上,四肢扭动,
那时我如何才能吐出
我平日生活方式的烟蒂?
  我哪敢冒昧行事?

我早就熟悉这些手臂,全都熟悉——
那戴手镯的白洁的裸臂,
(而灯光映出淡棕色的绒毛!)
是从衣衫上传来的香味
使我如此语无伦次?
是搁在桌上的,或裹着纱巾的手臂。
  难道我必须冒昧行事?
  叫我如何开始?

   * * * *

我该不该说,在暮色中我穿过狭窄的街道
看到没穿外套的孤独者倚在窗边
他的烟斗中升起缕缕白烟?……

我想必是一双褴褛的爪子
在宁静的海底乱窜。

   * * * *

And the afternoon, the evening, sleeps so peacefully!
Smoothed by long fingers,
Asleep... tired... or it malingers,
Stretched on the floor, here beside you and me.
Should I, after tea and cakes and ices,
Have the strength to force the moment to its crisis?
But though I have wept and fasted, wept and prayed,
Though I have seen my head (grown slightly bald)
    brought in upon a platter,
I am no prophet—and here's no great matter;
I have seen the moment of my greatness flicker,
And I have seen the eternal Footman hold my coat,
    and snicker,
And in short, I was afraid.

And would it have been worth it, after all,
After the cups, the marmalade, the tea,
Among the porcelain, among some talk of you and
    me,
Would it have been worth while,
To have bitten off the matter with a smile,
To have squeezed the universe into a ball
To roll it toward some overwhelming question,
To say: "I am Lazarus, come from the dead,

而这下午，这夜晚，睡得多安宁！

细长的手指抚摸着它，

睡着了……倦了……要不就是装病，

在你我身边，在地板上伸展四肢。

难道我在用过茶点和冷食之后

就有力量把时间推上紧要关头？

尽管我哭着斋戒过，哭着祈祷过，

尽管我见到我的脑袋（有些秃顶）放在盘里端来[1]，

我也不是先知——而这也并无大碍；

我已经见到我的伟大时刻闪闪摇摇，

我见到永生的男仆[2]拿着我的大衣向我冷笑，

一句话，我怕。

归根到底，这是否值得一做？

端杯喝茶，吃过果酱，

在杯盘之间，在你我闲谈时，

是否值得面带微笑

把这事情一口咬掉？

是否值得把宇宙挤成一个球

滚向一个叫人无法回答的问题，

是否值得说："我是拉撒路[3]，来自阴间，

---

1 据《新约·马太福音》施洗者约翰拒绝莎乐美的勾引，莎乐美诱使暴君希罗（一称希律）将约翰砍了头，把头放在盘子里端上来。
2 命运之神或死神。
3 据《圣经》，耶稣让拉撒路死后复活。

Come back to tell you all, I shall tell you all"—
If one, settling a pillow by her head,

    Should say: "That is not what I meant at all;
    That is not it, at all."

And would it have been worth it, after all,
Would it have been worth while,
After the sunsets and the dooryards and the sprinkled streets,
After the novels, after the teacups, after the skirts that trail along the floor—
And this, and so much more?—
It is impossible to say just what I mean!
But as if a magic lantern threw the nerves in patterns on a screen:
Would it have been worth while
If one, settling a pillow or throwing off a shawl,
And turning toward the window, should say:

    "That is not it at all,
    That is not what I meant, at all."

        * * * *

No! I am not Prince Hamlet, nor was meant to be;
Am an attendant lord, one that will do
To swell a progress, start a scene or two,
Advise the prince; no doubt, an easy tool,

我回来告诉你们一切,我要告诉你们一切"——
万一此人,在头边放个枕垫,
  竟然说:"我根本无此意,
  根本不是这么回事。"

归根到底,这是否值得一做?
是否值得,
经过庭院、洒水的街道、多次日落,
经过小说、茶杯、曳地长裙,
经过这个那个,还经过那么多事——
简直没法说出我想说的意思!
但就像魔灯把神经图案映到幕上:
是否还值得一做
万一此人,放下枕头,甩开纱巾,
朝窗子扭过脸,竟然说:
  "完全不是这么回事,
  我完全无此意,根本没这意思。"

* * * *

不!我不是哈姆雷特王子,生来不是,
我只是个扈从的廷臣,我的工作
只是让王家行列壮观些,念念开场白,
给王子出主意;当然,是驯顺的工具,

Deferential, glad to be of use,
Politic, cautious, and meticulous;
Full of high sentence, but a bit obtuse;
At times, indeed, almost ridiculous—
Almost, at times, the Fool.

I grow old... I grow old...
I shall wear the bottoms of my trousers rolled.

Shall I part my hair behind? Do I dare to eat a peach?
I shall wear white flannel trousers, and walk upon
  the beach.
I have heard the mermaids singing, each to each.

I do not think that they will sing to me.

I have seen them riding seaward on the waves
Combing the white hair of the waves blown back
When the wind blows the water white and black.

We have lingered in the chambers of the sea
By sea-girls wreathed with seaweed red and brown
Till human voices wake us, and we drown.

                                        1917

唯唯诺诺，很高兴终得一用，
处世小心，事事谨慎；
满嘴高调，却颇为颠顸，
有时候，确实，近乎可笑——
有时，几乎是小丑。[1]

我老了……我老了……
我得翻卷裤脚。

我脑后头发要不要两边分？[2] 我敢不敢吃桃子？
我要穿白色呢裤，在海滨漫步，
我听到了美人鱼对唱的歌声。

我想她们不会是唱给我听。

我见到她们骑在浪尖向大海驰去，
梳理着波浪被风吹起的长鬃，
这时风把海水扰得黑白相混。

我们在大海的宫室里流连忘返，
海女们给我们戴上红棕色海草花环，
一旦被人声唤醒，我们就得淹死。

1917

---

[1] 这一段中普鲁弗洛克自比《哈姆雷特》一剧中的廷臣波罗尼乌斯（Polonius）。

[2] 裤脚卷边和梳分头是20世纪初刚流行的时髦式样。

Preludes

I

The winter evening settles down
With smell of steaks in passageways.
Six o'clock.
The burnt-out ends of smoky days.
And now a gusty shower wraps
The grimy scraps
Of withered leaves about your feet
And newspapers from vacant lots;
The showers beat
On broken blinds and chimney-pots,
And at the corner of the street
A lonely cab-horse steams and stamps.

And then the lighting of the lamps.

1917

序曲[1]

冬夜带着牛排味
凝固在过道里。
六点整。
烟腾腾的白天烧剩的烟蒂。
而现在阵雨骤然
把萎黄的落叶那污秽的碎片
还有从空地上吹来的报纸
裹卷在自己脚边。
阵雨敲击着
破碎的百叶窗和烟囱管,
在街道转弯
一匹孤独的马冒着热气刨着蹄,

然后路灯一下子亮起。

1917

---

[1]《序曲》共包括四首短诗,这是第一首。

La Figlia Che Piange

O quam te memorem virgo...

Stand on the highest pavement of the stair—
Lean on a garden urn—
Weave, weave the sunlight in your hair—
Clasp your flowers to you with a pained surprise—
Fling them to the ground and turn
With a fugitive resentment in your eyes:
But weave, weave the sunlight in your hair.

So I would have had him leave,
So I would have had her stand and grieve,
So he would have left
As the soul leaves the body torn and bruised,
As the mind deserts the body it has used.
I should find
Some way incomparably light and deft,
Some way we both should understand,
Simple and faithless as a smile and a shake of the hand.

She turned away, but with the autumn weather

哭泣的姑娘 [1]

哦姑娘你叫什么…… [2]

站在楼梯顶的平台上——
靠着花盆——
织啊,在你的头发里编织阳光——
痛苦而惊奇,你把花抓起
扔到地上,转过身
眼中含着难以猜透的怒意:
但是织呵,在你的头发里编织阳光。

因此我但愿他走开,
因此我但愿她站着忧伤,
因此他但愿自己不在
好像灵魂离开遍体鳞伤的肉体,
好像理智把用旧的肉体抛弃。
我得找到
一种方法,无比轻捷巧妙,
一种方法,我俩都能理解,
简单,不确定,像握手,像微笑。

她转身走了,但随着这秋日天气,

---

[1] 原文为意大利语。
[2] 原引诗为拉丁语,引自维吉尔《伊尼德》(又称《埃涅阿斯记》)卷一,第327行。

Compelled my imagination many days,

Many days and many hours:

Her hair over her arms and her arms full of flowers.

And I wonder how they should have been together!

I should have lost a gesture and a pose.

Sometimes these cogitations still amaze

The troubled midnight, and the noon's repose.

1917

Morning at the Window

They are rattling breakfast plates in basement kitchens,

And along the trampled edges of the street

I am aware of the damp souls of housemaids

Sprouting despondently at area gates.

The brown waves of fog toss up to me

Twisted faces from the bottom of the street,

And tear from a passer-by with muddy skirts

An aimless smile that hovers in the air

And vanishes along the level of the roofs.

1917

好多天,追逼我的想象,
好多天,好多时光:
她臂上披着头发,手里抱着鲜花。
我真不明白他们怎能在一起!
怕是我丢失了一个姿态,一个手势。
有时这些想法仍然能惊起
苦恼的半夜与安宁的正午。

1917

窗前晨景

地下厨房里早餐盘子哗哗响,
而沿着行人践踏的街道两边,
我觉察到女佣人潮湿的灵魂
在大门口沮丧地冒出嫩芽。

晨雾的黄色波浪从街道底上
向我抛来一个个扭歪的面孔,
从穿脏裙子的路人脸上撕下
一个无目的的笑,让它飘在空中
沿着屋檐的水平方向渐渐消失。

1917

Aunt Helen

Miss Helen Slingsby was my maiden aunt,
And lived in a small house near a fashionable square
Cared for by servants to the number of four.
Now when she died there was silence in heaven
And silence at her end of the street.
The shutters were drawn and the undertaker wiped his feet—
He was aware that this sort of thing had occurred before.
The dogs were handsomely provided for,
But shortly afterwards the parrot died too.
The Dresden clock continued ticking on the mantelpiece,
And the footman sat upon the dining-table
Holding the second housemaid on his knees—
Who had always been so careful while her mistress lived.

1917

海伦姑妈

我的姑妈老处女海伦·斯林斯比,
住在豪华广场旁一幢小房子里,
四个仆人照顾她的起居,
现在她死了,天堂一片宁静,
她住的那个街头也是寂然无声。
百叶窗关了,殡仪馆老板掸掸鞋灰——
他很明白这种事情远非第一回。
狗的供应照常是相当丰盛,
但是不多久鹦鹉却也死去。
德累斯顿壁钟仍在炉架上滴答,
此时跟班却坐到餐桌边上,
把第二个侍女搂在膝盖上——
女主人生前她却是一贯谨慎。

1917

The Hippopotamus

The broad-backed hippopotamus
Rests on his belly in the mud;
Although he seems so firm to us
He is merely flesh and blood.

Flesh-and-blood is weak and frail,
Susceptible to nervous shock;
While the True Church can never fail
For it is based upon a rock.

The hippo's feeble steps may err
In compassing material ends,
While the True Church need never stir
To gather in its dividends.

The 'potamus can never reach
The mango on the mango-tree;
But fruits of pomegranate and peach
Refresh the Church from over sea.

At mating time the hippo's voice
Betrays inflexions hoarse and odd,

河马

那河马背宽肩广,
躺着,肚子贴紧烂泥。
我们看来他挺结实,
却也是血肉之躯。

血肉总是脆弱疲软,
易受神经冲动影响。
而真正教会从来不垮,
基础建在岩石之上。

河马会脚软,会闪跌,
当他要争取物质目的,
真正教会不必动弹,
就可坐收红利债息。

河马向来没法够着
树上长的累累芒果,
而海外运来石榴、鲜桃,
真正教会尝得快活。

在交配时河马的嗓子
吼出沙哑古怪的曲折,

But every week we hear rejoice
The Church, at being one with God.

The hippopotamus's day
Is passed in sleep; at night he hunts;
God works in a mysterious way—
The Church can sleep and feed at once.

I saw the 'potamus take wing
Ascending from the damp savannas,
And quiring angels round him sing
The praise of God, in loud hosannas.

Blood of the Lamb shall wash him clean
And him shall heavenly arms enfold,
Among the saints he shall be seen
Performing on a harp of gold.

He shall be washed as white as snow,
By all the martyr'd virgins kist,
While the True Church remains below
Wrapt in the old miasmal mist.

1920

但是教会每个周末
跟上帝结合多么欢乐。

河马在睡梦中
打发白天,夜里觅食,
而上帝行事相当神秘:
真正教会边睡边吃。

我看到河马飞升起来,
离开那卑湿的草原。
一群天使围护着他
齐唱着把上帝礼赞。

羔羊的血会把他洗净
怀抱着他的是神圣的手,
他将站在天使中间
把黄金的竖琴弹奏。

他将被洗得雪一样白
殉难的处女将他亲吻,
而真正教会留在下界
被古老的瘴雾妖氛笼罩。

1920

Whispers of Immortality (Excerpts)

Webster was much possessed by death
And saw the skull beneath the skin;
And breastless creatures under ground
Leaned backward with a lipless grin.

Daffodil bulbs instead of balls
Stared from the sockets of the eyes!
He knew that thought clings round dead limbs
Tightening its lusts and luxuries.

Donne, I suppose, was such another
Who found no substitute for sense;
To seize and clutch and penetrate,
Expert beyond experience,

He knew the anguish of the marrow
The ague of the skeleton;
No contact possible to flesh
Allayed the fever of the bone.

1920

不朽的低语 [1]（选段）

魏伯斯特 [2] 老想着死
在皮肤下面看到骷髅；
看到地下没有乳房的生物
带着无嘴唇的笑，仰身向后。

水仙的球根代替了眼珠，
从眼窝里朝外凝视！
他懂得思想缠住死人手足
收紧了它的淫欲和奢侈！

邓恩 [3]，我觉得，也是如此，
他认为无物能把感觉替代，
会抓捕，会掐紧，会穿透，
独具只眼，远在经验之外。

他了解骨髓的痛楚，
以及骨架的痉挛颤抖，
无论怎样去接触肉体
都无法医治发烧的骨头。

1920

---

1 本诗分两部分，这是第一部分。
2 约翰·魏伯斯特（约 1580—约 1634），英国文艺复兴后期悲剧作家。
3 约翰·邓恩（1572—1631），英国文艺复兴后期"玄学派"诗歌代表人物。

Sweeney Among the Nightingales

ὤμοι, πέπληγμαι καιρίαν πληγὴν ἔσω.

Apeneck Sweeney spreads his knees
Letting his arms hang down to laugh,
The zebra stripes along his jaw
Swelling to maculate giraffe.

The circles of the stormy moon
Slide westward toward the River Plate,
Death and the Raven drift above
And Sweeney guards the horned gate.

Gloomy Orion and the Dog
Are veiled; and hushed the shrunken seas;
The person in the Spanish cape
Tries to sit on Sweeney's knees

Slips and pulls the table cloth
Overturns a coffee-cup,
Reorganized upon the floor
She yawns and draws a stocking up;

斯威尼在夜莺之间

"啊,这一下要了我的命。" [1]

阿配奈克·斯威尼 [2] 两膝分开
手臂悬下,放声大笑,
斑马的花纹沿着下巴
肿胀成长颈鹿的色条。

预示风暴的一圈圈月晕,
向西,朝拉普拉塔河 [3] 滑行,
死神和乌鸦星在空中飘浮,
斯威尼守卫着角门 [4]。

阴郁的猎户座和天狼星
暗淡了,吓静了退缩的大海;
穿着西班牙斗篷的人
想坐上斯威尼的膝盖。

滑倒了,又拖下了桌布
翻倒杯子,倾洒咖啡,
她在地板上整顿一番,
打呵欠,把袜子拉上腿;

---

[1] 原文为希腊文,引自埃斯库罗斯的戏剧《阿伽门农》,阿伽门农被其妻谋害,这是他临死前说的话。
[2] 斯威尼是艾略特诗中常用的一个人名。
[3] 南美洲的一条河。
[4] 希腊神话中,角门是梦从地下世界进入人世必经的门。

The silent man in mocha brown
Sprawls at the window-sill and gapes;
The waiter brings in oranges
Bananas figs and hothouse grapes;

The silent vertebrate in brown
Contracts and concentrates, withdraws;
Rachel née Rabinovitch
Tears at the grapes with murderous paws;

She and the lady in the cape
Are suspect, thought to be in league;
Therefore the man with heavy eyes
Declines the gambit, shows fatigue,

Leaves the room and reappears
Outside the window, leaning in,
Branches of wistaria
Circumscribe a golden grin;

The host with someone indistinct
Converses at the door apart,
The nightingales are singing near
The Convent of the Sacred Heart,

穿咖色上衣的男人一声不吭
张着大口扒在窗前。
侍者送进橘子,还有
那些无花果、香蕉和葡萄干;

穿棕衣的脊椎动物一声不吭
畏畏缩缩,往后退开;
而拉契尔,娘家姓拉比诺维契
伸出爪子把葡萄撕碎;

她和那个披斗篷的太太
有嫌疑,看来勾结一气;
因此那个眼色沉重的男人
装出疲倦样子,拒绝开局,

离开房间,却在窗外,
重新出现,身子往里探,
那紫藤树的枝枝叶叶
把金色的狂笑团团围环;

主人与一个难辨认的人,
在打开的窗口交谈,
在圣心修道院近旁
有夜莺歌喉婉转,

And sang within the bloody wood

When Agamemnon cried aloud,

And let their liquid siftings fall

To stain the stiff dishonoured shroud.

1920

Gerontion

Thou hast nor youth nor age
But as it were an after dinner sleep
Dreaming of both.

Here I am, an old man in a dry month,

Being read to by a boy, waiting for rain.

I was neither at the hot gates

Nor fought in the warm rain

Nor knee deep in the salt marsh, heaving a cutlass,

Bitten by flies, fought.

My house is a decayed house,

它们在血污的树丛歌唱
当阿伽门农大声号啕,[1]
它们让血液滴滴筛下
弄脏僵硬的可耻尸袍。

1920

小老头[2]

你既无青春又无老年
但在午餐后的小憩里,
你梦见了两者。[3]

这是我,旱季里一个老人,
等着下雨,让个男孩念书给我听。
我既不是站在热门[4]前,
也不是在暖雨中挣扎,
也没有陷进盐沼,被虻虫叮咬
挥舞短剑做殊死一斗。
我的房子行将倾圮

---

1 据埃斯库罗斯的悲剧,阿伽门农被其妻用斧子砍死。"血污的树丛",据艾略特自己解释,指索福克勒斯《俄狄浦斯在科罗诺斯》一剧中写到的"怨灵们"居住的树丛,树丛里面有夜莺歌唱。
2 原标题为希腊文。
3 引自莎士比亚《量罪记》第三幕第一场,公爵用这些话劝面临死刑的克劳狄奥不要把生命看得太重。
4 热门,即温泉关,希腊中部与北部之间的一个隘口,军事要地,公元前480年希腊与波斯军队曾在此激战。

And the jew squats on the window sill, the owner,

Spawned in some estaminet of Antwerp,

Blistered in Brussels, patched and peeled in London.

The goat coughs at night in the field overhead;

Rocks, moss, stonecrop, iron, merds.

The woman keeps the kitchen, makes tea,

Sneezes at evening, poking the peevish gutter.

  I an old man,

A dull head among windy spaces.

Signs are taken for wonders. "We would see a sign":

The word within a word, unable to speak a word,

Swaddled with darkness. In the juvescence of the year

Came Christ the tiger

In depraved May, dogwood and chestnut, flowering judas,

To be eaten, to be divided, to be drunk

Among whispers; by Mr. Silvero

With caressing hands, at Limoges

Who walked all night in the next room;

1　"下子儿"暗指混乱的性生活,"长水泡"等指性病。"山羊"在西方被认为是性能力的象征,山羊咳嗽,指性无能。

2　典出《新约·马太福音》第12章。不信上帝的法利赛人要耶稣拿出证明,证实他的确是上帝之子,他们说:"我们要看神迹。"耶稣回答说:"一个邪恶淫乱的世代求看神迹。"

而犹太人，那房东，蹲在窗台上，

在安特卫普一家小酒馆下子儿，

在布鲁塞尔长水泡，在伦敦脱皮、贴膏药，

半夜山羊在上面的田野里咳嗽，[1]

岩石、苔藓、景天、铁、粪便。

女人掌厨，准备茶点，

晚上打喷嚏，挑旺乖戾的火。

   我只是个老人

刮风的空间中一个愚钝的头脑。

征兆被当作奇迹。"我们要看神迹"[2]：

言词中之言词，说不出言词

裹在黑暗中的言词。在大地还春之时

来了基督，那老虎[3]

在腐烂的五月，有山茱萸和栗子，有开花的紫荆，

可以分给大家在悄声低语中吃喝，[4]

分吃的人有西尔维罗先生，

他的手很温柔，在利摩日[5]

整夜在隔壁房间徘徊；

---

3 典出英国诗人威廉·布莱克（1757—1827）的名诗《老虎》，布莱克用"老虎"象征上帝的力量和愤怒。
4 指耶稣在最后的晚餐时把面包和酒作为自己的身体和血的象征物分给门徒们吃喝。
5 法国一城市名。

By Hakagawa, bowing among the Titians;
By Madame de Tornquist, in the dark room
Shifting the candles; Fräulein von Kulp
Who turned in the hall, one hand on the door.
      Vacant shuttles
Weave the wind. I have no ghosts,
An old man in a draughty house
Under a windy knob.

After such knowledge, what forgiveness? Think now
History has many cunning passages, contrived corridors
And issues, deceives with whispering ambitions,
Guides us by vanities. Think now
She gives when our attention is distracted
And what she gives, gives with such supple confusions
That the giving famishes the craving. Gives too late
What's not believed in, or if still believed,
In memory only, reconsidered passion. Gives too soon
Into weak hands, what's thought can be dispensed with
Till the refusal propagates a fear. Think
Neither fear nor courage saves us. Unnatural vices
Are fathered by our heroism. Virtues

还有冢川先生,他在提香的画之间鞠躬

还有董魁斯特夫人,在黑房间里

换蜡烛;冯·库尔普小姐

走向大厅,一手搭在门上。

　空无所有的梭子

编织着风。我没见鬼,

一个老人坐在有穿堂风的房子里

头上是刮风的山丘。

知道了这种事,还有何谅宥可言?我想到

历史有许多诡秘的通道,精心安排的走廊

和出口,她用鬼鬼祟祟的野心欺骗我们

用虚荣引诱我们。想一想吧,

我们没留意时她塞东西给我们

而她给的东西都是混乱不堪

反使人更加心馋。给得太晚的东西

已没人相信,即使相信

也只是在回忆里,在重新唤起的激情中。而给得

　太早的东西

软弱的手接过来,却觉得可有可无

直到拒绝使人害怕。想一想吧

无论恐惧和勇气都救不了我们。我们的罪孽,

靠我们的英雄主义培育。

Are forced upon us by our impudent crimes.

These tears are shaken from the wrath-bearing tree.

The tiger springs in the new year. Us he devours. Think at last
We have not reached conclusion, when I
Stiffen in a rented house. Think at last
I have not made this show purposelessly
And it is not by any concitation
Of the backward devils
I would meet you upon this honestly.
I that was near your heart was removed therefrom
To lose beauty in terror, terror in inquisition.
I have lost my passion: why should I need to keep it
Since what is kept must be adulterated?
I have lost my sight, smell, hearing, taste and touch:
How should I use them for your closer contact?

These with a thousand small deliberations
Protract the profit of their chilled delirium,
Excite the membrane, when the sense has cooled,
With pungent sauces, multiply variety
In a wilderness of mirrors. What will the spider do,
Suspend its operations, will the weevil

而我们厚颜的劣迹,却强加给我们美德。

这些眼泪都是从长着愤怒之果的树上摇下来的。

老虎在新的一年跃起,吞吃我们。[1]

 ·最后想一想吧

我们还没得出结论,而我已经

在租来的房子里全身僵直。最后再想一想吧

我并不是毫无目的出乖露丑,

这也不是后退的魔鬼们

搞出来的一场虚惊。

我将正大光明地与你们谈这问题。

我的心原先离你那么近,现在被拉远。

在恐怖中失去美,在寻求中失去恐怖。

我丧失了热情,我又何必要保存热情,

既然保存的东西全得掺假?

我失去了视觉、嗅觉、听觉、味觉和触觉:

我还能用什么感觉与你接触?

这些,还有成千细枝末节的考虑

延长了他们冻僵了的梦呓的好处

当感觉已冷却,它们用刺鼻的酱油

来刺激黏膜,无数的镜子

添出各种映象。蜘蛛将干什么?

它会暂时停止行动?象鼻虫会不会

---

[1] 按基督教仪式,教徒在圣诞节吃象征耶稣血肉的圣餐,在"小老头"看来事情正好相反。

Delay? De Bailhache, Fresca, Mrs. Cammel, whirled
Beyond the circuit of the shuddering Bear
In fractured atoms. Gull against the wind, in the
  windy straits
Of Belle Isle, or running on the Horn,
White feathers in the snow, the Gulf claims,
And an old man driven by the Trades
To a sleepy corner.

        Tenants of the house,
Thoughts of a dry brain in a dry season.

                                             1920

The Waste Land

"*Nam Sibyllam quidem Cumis ego ipse oculis meis vidi in ampulla pendere, et cum illi pueri dicerent: Σιβυλλα τι θελεις; respondebat illa: αποθανειν θελω.*"

               for Ezra Pound
               il miglior fabbro.

逡巡踌躇？¹ 德·培拉希，弗雷斯卡

和卡墨尔太太²越过大熊星的圈子，

在破裂的原子中旋转。而海燕

在狂风呼啸的贝尔岛³海峡或合恩角⁴上空疾飞，

海湾索求雪中的白羽毛，

信风吹送一个老人

送他到安睡的角落。

  屋子的住户，

干燥季节干枯头脑里的思想。

1920

荒原

"我曾亲眼看见库迈的西比尔挂在瓶中，当孩子们问她：'西比尔，你要什么？'她回答说：'我要死。'"

献给埃兹拉·庞德

最杰出的艺人

---

1 "蜘蛛""象鼻虫"等等，指尸体交付给蛆虫。
2 这是随意取的名字。
3 加拿大东部海岸一地名。
4 南美洲最南端合恩岛上的南角。

I. The Burial of the Dead

April is the cruellest month, breeding

Lilacs out of the dead land, mixing

Memory and desire, stirring

Dull roots with spring rain.

Winter kept us warm, covering

Earth in forgetful snow, feeding

A little life with dried tubers.

Summer surprised us, coming over the Starnbergersee

With a shower of rain; we stopped in the colonnade,

And went on in sunlight, into the Hofgarten,   10

And drank coffee, and talked for an hour.

Bin gar keine Russin, stamm' aus Litauen, echt deutsch.

And when we were children, staying at the arch-duke's,

My cousin's, he took me out on a sled,

And I was frightened. He said, Marie,

Marie, hold on tight. And down we went.

In the mountains, there you feel free.

I read, much of the night, and go south in the winter.

     What are the roots that clutch, what branches grow

Out of this stony rubbish? Son of man,   20

You cannot say, or guess, for you know only

A heap of broken images, where the sun beats,

一、死者葬仪

四月是最残酷的月份，在死地上

养育出丁香，扰混了

回忆和欲望，用春雨

惊醒迟钝的根。

冬天使我们温暖，用健忘的雪

把大地覆盖，用干瘪的根茎

喂养微弱的生命。

夏天使人吃惊，它越过施坦贝格湖

带来暴雨；我们在柱廊里躲了一阵，

(10) 天晴了继续朝前走，进了皇家花园，

我们喝咖啡，聊了一小时。

我不是俄国女人，我生在立陶宛，真正的德国人

我们小时候，在表哥，

大公爵家里小住，他带我坐雪橇，

我胆战心惊。他说，玛丽，

玛丽，抓紧，于是我们往下滑。

在山里，你感到自由。

我看书常到深夜，冬天我去南方。

　　什么树根在紧攫？什么树枝

(20) 从石头垃圾中长出？人子啊，

你说不出，猜不着，因为你只认识

一大堆破碎的形象，那里赤日炎炎，

And the dead tree gives no shelter, the cricket no
    relief,
And the dry stone no sound of water. Only
There is shadow under this red rock,
(Come in under the shadow of this red rock),
And I will show you something different from either
Your shadow at morning striding behind you
Or your shadow at evening rising to meet you;
I will show you fear in a handful of dust.   30

    Frisch weht der Wind

    Der Heimat zu.

    Mein Irisch Kind,

    Wo weilest du?

"You gave me hyacinths first a year ago;
"They called me the hyacinth girl."
—Yet when we came back, late, from the Hyacinth
    garden,
Your arms full, and your hair wet, I could not
Speak, and my eyes failed, I was neither
Living nor dead, and I knew nothing,   40
Looking into the heart of light, the silence.

    Oed' und leer das Meer.

    Madame Sosostris, famous clairvoyante,
Had a bad cold, nevertheless

死树下没有阴凉，虫鸣不让人轻松，
干石头上没有淙淙泉音，只有
这块红石投下的阴影，
（到这阴影中来吧）
我会给你看个东西，既不同于
早晨在你身后阔步的影子，也不同于
晚上升起来迎接你的影子；
(30) 我给你看一捧尘土中的恐惧。

清凉的风啊

吹我回家乡，

我的爱尔兰姑娘

你流连在何方？

"一年前你第一次给我玉簪花；
他们叫我玉簪女郎。"
——可是当我们从玉簪花园晚归，
你满抱着花，头发沾湿，我却口舌
难言，两眼模糊，不死
(40) 也不活，一无所知，
窥看着光芒中心那一片寂静。

茫茫沧海一望空阔。

索索特利斯太太，出名的相士
伤风挺厉害，然而却是

Is known to be the wisest woman in Europe,
With a wicked pack of cards. Here, said she,
Is your card, the drowned Phoenician Sailor,
(Those are pearls that were his eyes. Look!)
Here is Belladonna, the Lady of the Rocks,
The lady of situations.   50
Here is the man with three staves, and here the Wheel,
And here is the one-eyed merchant, and this card,
Which is blank, is something he carries on his back,
Which I am forbidden to see. I do not find
The Hanged Man. Fear death by water.
I see crowds of people, walking round in a ring.
Thank you. If you see dear Mrs. Equitone,
Tell her I bring the horoscope myself:
One must be so careful these days.

   Unreal City,   60
Under the brown fog of a winter dawn,
A crowd flowed over London Bridge, so many,
I had not thought death had undone so many.
Sighs, short and infrequent, were exhaled,
And each man fixed his eyes before his feet.
Flowed up the hill and down King William Street,
To where Saint Mary Woolnoth kept the hours
With a dead sound on the final stroke of nine.

全欧洲最睿智的女人,

有一副绝妙的纸牌。她说这一张

就是你的牌,淹死的腓尼基水手,

(这两颗珍珠是他的眼睛变的。瞧!)

这是颠茄花,礁岩美女,

(50) 　随机应变的女人。

这是带三根手杖的人,这是舵轮,

这是独眼商人,而这张

空白的牌,他扛在背上的东西

是不许我看的。我找不到

"倒吊人"那张牌。当心死在水里。

我看到一群群人绕圈儿走。

谢谢。你见到依奎东太太

就告诉她天宫图我自己带去,

这年头真得事事小心。

(60) 　　　虚幻的城市

冬晨的棕色烟雾下

人群涌过伦敦桥,那么多人,

我想不到死神毁了那么多人,

时而吐出短促的叹息,

每个人眼睛看定脚前,

涌上山,沿着威廉国王大街,

走向圣玛丽·乌尔诺斯教堂敲钟的地方,

钟敲九点,最后的一声死气沉沉。

There I saw one I knew, and stopped him, crying
"Stetson!
"You who were with me in the ships at Mylae!   70
"That corpse you planted last year in your garden,
"Has it begun to sprout? Will it bloom this year?
"Or has the sudden frost disturbed its bed?
"Oh keep the Dog far hence, that's friend to men,
"Or with his nails he'll dig it up again!
"You! hypocrite lecteur!—mon semblable,—mon
    frère!"

II. A Game of Chess

The Chair she sat in, like a burnished throne,
Glowed on the marble, where the glass
Held up by standards wrought with fruited vines
From which a golden Cupidon peeped out   80
(Another hid his eyes behind his wing)
Doubled the flames of seven branched candelabra
Reflecting light upon the table as
The glitter of her jewels rose to meet it,
From satin cases poured in rich profusion;
In vials of ivory and coloured glass
Unstoppered, lurked her strange synthetic perfumes,
Unguent, powdered, or liquid—troubled, confused
And drowned the sense in odours; stirred by the air

我见到一个熟人,我拦住他喊道:"斯特曾!

(70) 在迈利我们俩在一条舰上!

去年你在花园里种下的尸体

开始抽芽了吗?今年能开花?

来得突然的寒霜没冻毁它的床?

哦,别让狗靠近,他是人的朋友,

要不然它会用爪子把尸体挖出来!

你!虚伪的读者!——我的同类!——我的兄弟!"

二、一局棋

她坐的椅子,像擦亮的王座,

在大理石台基上闪闪发光,镜子的

支座上雕着串串累累的葡萄,

(80) 后面有个金色的小爱神探头探脑,

(另一个用翅膀遮住眼睛,)

镜子使七枝烛架倍添光焰,

把光线反射在桌面上,

而她的缎衬首饰匣里涌出的

珠光宝气迎着烛光升起;

开着盖子的象牙和彩色玻璃

小瓶里,藏着她奇异的合成香料,

香膏、香粉、香水——扰乱了嗅觉,

把它淹没在各种香味里,而窗外扑进

That freshened from the window, these ascended 90
In fattening the prolonged candle-flames,
Flung their smoke into the laquearia,
Stirring the pattern on the coffered ceiling.
Huge sea-wood fed with copper
Burned green and orange, framed by the coloured
    stone,
In which sad light a carvèd dolphin swam.
Above the antique mantel was displayed
As though a window gave upon the sylvan scene
The change of Philomel, by the barbarous king
So rudely forced; yet there the nightingale 100
Filled all the desert with inviolable voice
And still she cried, and still the world pursues,
"Jug Jug" to dirty ears.
And other withered stumps of time
Were told upon the walls; staring forms
Leaned out, leaning, hushing the room enclosed.
Footsteps shuffled on the stair.
Under the firelight, under the brush, her hair
Spread out in fiery points
Glowed into words, then would be savagely still. 110

    "My nerves are bad to-night. Yes, bad. Stay with me.
"Speak to me. Why do you never speak? Speak.

(90)　　　新鲜空气，吹动香气，它们上升
　　　　　吹旺了拉长的烛焰，
　　　　　把烟抛上镶嵌天花板，
　　　　　模糊了天花板的方格，
　　　　　海水浸过的柴，撒着铜粉，
　　　　　闪出绿色橙色的光，而在惨戚的光里
　　　　　彩色石框中游着雕刻的海豚。
　　　　　在古色古香的壁炉架上
　　　　　好像窗子对着山林景色
　　　　　费洛美拉变了形，被野蛮的国王
(100)　　 如此残暴地蹂躏；但是夜莺
　　　　　仍在用不可凌辱的声音填满荒漠，
　　　　　她仍在向着肮脏的耳朵喊着
　　　　　"啾，啾"，而世界今天还在追逼。
　　　　　其他枯萎的时间的残株
　　　　　在墙上写下标记；雕像瞪着眼
　　　　　探身，向前，要关着的房间保持静穆。
　　　　　楼梯上传来拖着脚走的声音。
　　　　　在灯光下，在刷子下，她的头发
　　　　　闪着火一般的光点铺展开来
(110)　　 燃烧成话语，又变成野蛮的沉静。

　　　　　"今夜我情绪不好。真的，很不好。留下陪我。
　　　　　跟我说话。为什么你老不开口？说呀！

"What are you thinking of? What thinking? What?
"I never know what you are thinking. Think."

    I think we are in rats' alley
Where the dead men lost their bones.

"What is that noise?"
                The wind under the door.
"What is that noise now? What is the wind doing?"
                Nothing again nothing.   120
                      "Do
"You know nothing? Do you see nothing? Do you
   remember
"Nothing?"

    I remember
Those are pearls that were his eyes.
"Are you alive, or not? Is there nothing in your head?"

                    But
O O O O that Shakespeherian Rag—
It's so elegant
So intelligent   130
"What shall I do now? What shall I do?"
"I shall rush out as I am, and walk the street

你在想什么？想什么？什么？
我老是不明白你在想什么。想吧。"

  我想我们正在老鼠的巷子里，
这里死人连骨头都剩不下来。

"这是什么声音？"
      门下有风。
"这又是什么声音？风在干吗？"
(120)   没什么，什么也没有。
      "你真的
什么也不知道？什么也没看见？
什么也不记得？"

  我记得
这两颗珍珠是他的眼睛变的。
"你还活着？还是死了？你头脑里什么也没有？"

      可是
哦哦哦哦这莎士比亚式的爵士乐
  如此雅致
(130) 如此机灵
"我现在有什么事可做？有什么事可做？
我就这样冲出去，走到街上，

"With my hair down, so. What shall we do to-morrow?
"What shall we ever do?"
                              The hot water at ten.
And if it rains, a closed car at four.
And we shall play a game of chess,
Pressing lidless eyes and waiting for a knock upon the
    door.

When Lil's husband got demobbed, I said—
I didn't mince my words, I said to her myself,   140
HURRY UP PLEASE ITS TIME
Now Albert's coming back, make yourself a bit smart.
He'll want to know what you done with that money
    he gave you
To get yourself some teeth. He did, I was there.
You have them all out, Lil, and get a nice set,
He said, I swear, I can't bear to look at you.
And no more can't I, I said, and think of poor Albert,
He's been in the army four years, he wants a good
    time,
And if you don't give it him, there's others will, I said.
Oh is there, she said. Something o' that, I said.   150
Then I'll know who to thank, she said, and give me
    a straight look.

头发披散，就这样。明天我们干什么？

我们究竟能干什么？"

         上午十点来热水。

要是下雨，四点钟会来辆有篷的汽车。

我们将下一局棋，

按着没眼皮的眼睛，等着敲门声。

莉尔的丈夫退伍时，我说过——

(140) 我一点不含糊，亲口对她说的，

请赶紧点，时间到了

阿尔伯特快回来了，你要打扮得俏一些。

他会问给你的那些镶牙的钱

是怎么用掉的。他给了你钱，我在场。

把牙全换了吧，莉尔，换副漂亮的，

的的确确，他说过我受不了你这模样，

我也看不下去，我说，要为可怜的阿尔伯特着想，

他在军队里干了四年，现在想痛快一下，

你不给他痛快，别人会给，我说。

(150) 哦，是吗？她说。我说，就是这么回事。

她说，那我就知道该谢谁了，她白了我一眼。

HURRY UP PLEASE ITS TIME

If you don't like it you can get on with it, I said.

Others can pick and choose if you can't.

But if Albert makes off, it won't be for lack of telling.

You ought to be ashamed, I said, to look so antique.

(And her only thirty-one.)

I can't help it, she said, pulling a long face,

It's them pills I took, to bring it off, she said.

(She's had five already, and nearly died of young George.)

The chemist said it would be alright, but I've never been the same.

You *are* a proper fool, I said.

Well, if Albert won't leave you alone, there it is, I said,

What you get married for if you don't want children?

HURRY UP PLEASE ITS TIME

Well, that Sunday Albert was home, they had a hot gammon,

And they asked me in to dinner, to get the beauty of it hot—

HURRY UP PLEASE ITS TIME

HURRY UP PLEASE ITS TIME

Goonight Bill. Goonight Lou. Goonight May. Goonight.

请赶紧点，时间到了

你不乐意，可以就这么混下去，我说。

别人能挑挑拣拣，你可不行。

要是阿尔伯特找了别人，我可是警告过你的。

你看上去这么老，我说，真不害臊。

（她才三十一岁）

没法子，她说，拉长了脸，

全是那些打胎药片，她说。

(160) （她已经有过五次，差点死在小乔治手里）

药店老板说没事，可我觉得再不如从前。

你是个标准笨蛋，我说。

好吧，要是阿尔伯特不放过你，这事又会来，

你不想要孩子又何必结婚？

请赶紧点，时间到了

星期天，阿尔伯特到了家，他们大吃热火腿，

还叫我去吃饭，趁那热劲儿——

请赶紧点，时间到了

请赶紧点，时间到了

(170) 明儿见，比尔。明儿见，露。明儿见，梅。明儿见。

Ta ta. Goonight. Goonight.

Good night, ladies, good night, sweet ladies, good night, good night.

III. The Fire Sermon

The river's tent is broken: the last fingers of leaf
Clutch and sink into the wet bank. The wind
Crosses the brown land, unheard. The nymphs are departed.
Sweet Thames, run softly, till I end my song.
The river bears no empty bottles, sandwich papers,
Silk handkerchiefs, cardboard boxes, cigarette ends
Or other testimony of summer nights. The nymphs are departed.
And their friends, the loitering heirs of city directors;
Departed, have left no addresses.
By the waters of Leman I sat down and wept...
Sweet Thames, run softly till I end my song,
Sweet Thames, run softly, for I speak not loud or long.
But at my back in a cold blast I hear
The rattle of the bones, and chuckle spread from ear to ear.

回见。明儿见,明儿见。

明儿见,太太们,明儿见,好太太,明儿见,
　　明儿见。

三、火诫

河的帐篷已破:树叶临终的手指

揪紧着,陷入潮湿的河岸。而风

无人觉察,掠过棕黄色的大地。仙女们走了,

可爱的泰晤士河静静地流,直到我唱完歌。

河上看不见空瓶、三明治纸包、

绸手绢、纸匣、烟头,

看不到夏夜留下的痕迹。仙女们已离去,

(180)　她们的朋友,市政要员懒散的继承人

也走了,没留下地址。

在莱芒的岸边,我坐下来哭泣……

可爱的泰晤士河,静静地流,直到我唱完歌,

可爱的泰晤士河,静静地流,我不大声,也不
　　多说。

可是在我背后,冷风骤起,我听到

骨头咔咔嗒嗒碰响,拉开大嘴的冷笑。

A rat crept softly through the vegetation
Dragging its slimy belly on the bank
While I was fishing in the dull canal
On a winter evening round behind the gashouse   190
Musing upon the king my brother's wreck
And on the king my father's death before him.
White bodies naked on the low damp ground
And bones cast in a little low dry garret,
Rattled by the rat's foot only, year to year.
But at my back from time to time I hear
The sound of horns and motors, which shall bring
Sweeney to Mrs. Porter in the spring.
O the moon shone bright on Mrs. Porter
And on her daughter   200
They wash their feet in soda water
Et, O ces voix d'enfants, chantant dans la coupole!

    Twit twit twit
Jug jug jug jug jug jug
So rudely forc'd.
Tereu

    Unreal City
Under the brown fog of a winter noon
Mr. Eugenides, the Smyrna merchant

一只老鼠轻声从草丛中爬过,

黏糊糊的肚子在河岸上拖着,

而我却在一个冬夜,绕到煤气厂背后,

(190)　在死沉沉的运河中垂钓,

我沉思,想着我那做国王的兄弟覆舟遇难,

又想起在他之前,我的父王死去,

惨白的尸体赤裸地躺在潮湿的洼地上,

骨头却扔进了低矮干燥的阁楼,

年复一年,只有老鼠踢响骨头。

但是在我背后,我每隔一会就听到

喇叭声和马达声,在春天

这声音把斯威尼带到波特太太那儿去。

哦,月光朗照在波特太太身上,

(200)　朗照在她的女儿身上

她们在苏打水里洗脚

哦这些孩子的歌声,在教堂里唱!

　　啼啼啼

啾啾啾啾啾啾

如此粗暴地蹂躏

忒流

　　虚幻的城市

冬日正午的黄雾下

士麦那商人尤金尼德斯先生

Unshaven, with a pocket full of currants   210
C.i.f. London: documents at sight,
Asked me in demotic French
To luncheon at the Cannon Street Hotel
Followed by a weekend at the Metropole.

    At the violet hour, when the eyes and back
Turn upward from the desk, when the human engine
   waits
Like a taxi throbbing waiting,
I Tiresias, though blind, throbbing between two lives,
Old man with wrinkled female breasts, can see
At the violet hour, the evening hour that strives   220
Homeward, and brings the sailor home from sea,
The typist home at teatime, clears her breakfast, lights
Her stove, and lays out food in tins.
Out of the window perilously spread
Her drying combinations touched by the sun's last
   rays,
On the divan are piled (at night her bed)
Stockings, slippers, camisoles, and stays.
I Tiresias, old man with wrinkled dugs
Perceived the scene, and foretold the rest—
I too awaited the expected guest.   230
He, the young man carbuncular, arrives,

(210)   满脸胡子茬,袋里装着

"到岸价运伦敦,见票即付"的葡萄干

一口粗俗的法语,请我

在卡农街饭店吃午饭

再到"大都会"度周末。

    在紫色的黄昏,眼睛和背脊

从桌上抬起来,人体发动机等着

就像出租汽车马达跳着在等,

我,梯雷西亚斯,虽然眼瞎,心却跳在两个生

    命之间

我是个长着萎瘪女人乳房的老头,我能见到

(220) 在紫色的时辰,夜晚大步

往家里走,从大海带回来水手。

打字员回家喝茶,洗早餐碗盘,点燃

她的炉子,拿出罐头食品。

而窗外,惊险地展开

她晾的连裤亵衣,被残阳触摸着。

沙发(夜里当床)上面堆着

袜子、拖鞋、背心、乳罩。

我,梯雷西亚斯,乳房萎瘪的老头

看到这一切,也预告了下文——

(230) 我也在等那将要来的客人。

那满脸粉刺的青年人来了,

A small house agent's clerk, with one bold stare,
One of the low on whom assurance sits
As a silk hat on a Bradford millionaire.
The time is now propitious, as he guesses,
The meal is ended, she is bored and tired,
Endeavors to engage her in caresses
Which still are unreproved, if undesired.
Flushed and decided, he assaults at once;
Exploring hands encounter no defence;   240
His vanity requires no response,
And makes a welcome of indifference.
(And I Tiresias have foresuffered all
Enacted on this same divan or bed;
I who have sat by Thebes below the wall
And walked among the lowest of the dead.)
Bestows one final patronising kiss,
And gropes his way, finding the stairs unlit...

    She turns and looks a moment in the glass,
Hardly aware of her departed lover;   250
Her brain allows one half-formed thought to pass:
"Well now that's done: and I'm glad it's over."
When lovely woman stoops to folly and
Paces about her room again, alone,
She smoothes her hair with automatic hand,

房产公司的小职员，眼光却十分大胆，

一个下流角色，心里装着自信，

就像丝绒帽子戴在布拉德福德百万富翁头上。

他估计此刻时机绝佳，

打字员刚吃完饭，正感到腻烦，疲倦，

他使出功夫来与她亲热，

没挨骂，但也没受鼓励，

涨红了脸，下了决心，他立即进攻；

(240) 试探的手没有遇到阻挡；

他的自大使他不需要对方响应，

他反而喜欢这种冷漠的态度。

（而我，梯雷西亚斯，早就吃过这苦，

我就在这张沙发兼床上演过这出戏；

我曾在底比斯城墙下坐过，

也曾在最卑贱的死人中走过。）

他恩赐给她最后的一吻，

摸索着走出来，发现楼梯没点灯……

      她翻过身，朝镜子里看了一阵，

(250) 根本没去想那已经走掉的情人；

她脑子里只闪过一个半截子念头：

"总算完了。完了就好。"

可爱的女人屈身做了蠢事，

一个人在房间里来回踱步，

她用手机械地理理头发，顺手

And puts a record on the gramophone.

"This music crept by me upon the waters"
And along the Strand, up Queen Victoria Street.
O City city, I can sometimes hear
Beside a public bar in Lower Thames Street, 260
The pleasant whining of a mandoline
And a clatter and a chatter from within
Where fishmen lounge at noon: where the walls
Of Magnus Martyr hold
Inexplicable splendour of Ionian white and gold.

  The river sweats
 Oil and tar
 The barges drift
 With the turning tide
 Red sails 270
 Wide
 To leeward, swing on the heavy spar.
 The barges wash
 Drifting logs
 Down Greenwich reach
 Past the Isle of Dogs.
    Weialala leia
    Wallala leialala

在留声机上放张唱片。

"这音乐从我身边的水面上漂过"
沿着河滨街，穿过维多利亚女王街。
啊城市，城市，我有时能听见
(260)　在下泰晤士街一家酒馆旁
曼陀林琴声如怨如诉，
酒店里杯盘叮当，人声骚然，
是渔夫们中午在闲逛：就在那儿，殉道者教堂
墙壁上有一种难以解释的
白色与金色混杂的爱奥尼亚光华。

　　　　大河蒸腾着
　　焦油和沥青
　　潮水回头时
　　驳船顺水而去
(270)　红色的帆
　　张开着
　　顺风直下，在沉重的桅杆上摇晃。
　　驳船漂流
　　像巨大的木头
　　直到格林尼治河岸
　　经过多格斯岛。
　　　　　威啊啦啦列依啊
　　　　　威啦啦列依啊啦

> Elizabeth and Leicester
>
> Beating oars 280
>
> The stern was formed
>
> A gilded shell
>
> Red and gold
>
> The brisk swell
>
> Rippled both shores
>
> Southwest wind
>
> Carried down stream
>
> The peal of bells
>
> White towers
>
>> Weialala leia 290
>>
>> Wallala leialala

"Trams and dusty trees.
Highbury bore me. Richmond and Kew
Undid me. By Richmond I raised my knees
Supine on the floor of a narrow canoe."

"My feet are at Moorgate, and my heart
Under my feet. After the event
He wept. He promised 'a new start.'
I made no comment. What should I resent?"

　　　　　　伊丽莎白和莱斯特

(280)　　船桨击水

　　　　船尾的水花

　　　　像一枚镀金的贝壳

　　　　红色、金色

　　　　船冲起迅跑的波

　　　　拍上河岸

　　　　西南风吹来

　　　　阵阵钟响

　　　　白色的塔

　　　　带到下游

(290)　　　　　威啊啦啦列依啊
　　　　　　　威啦啦列依啊啦

　　"电车，蒙满灰尘的树。
海伯里养育了我，里士满和基尤
害了我。在里士满我抬起双膝
仰卧在小舟的舱板上。"

　　"我的脚在莫尔门，我的心
却在脚底。事情过后
他哭了。他保证'重新做人。'
我无话可说，我有什么可怨？"

> "On Margate Sands.   300
> I can connect
> Nothing with nothing.
> The broken fingernails of dirty hands.
> My people humble people who expect
> Nothing."
>   la la

To Carthage then I came

  Burning burning burning burning
O Lord Thou pluckest me out
O Lord Thou pluckest   310

burning

IV. Death by Water

Phlebas the Phoenician, a fortnight dead,
Forgot the cry of gulls, and the deep seas swell
And the profit and loss.
                    A current under sea
Picked his bones in whispers. As he rose and fell
He passed the stages of his age and youth
Entering the whirlpool.
                    Gentile or Jew

(300)   "在马盖特的沙滩

  我能把

  虚无与虚无联结起来。

  脏手的破指甲。

  我们,卑贱的人,毫无

  指望。"

    啦啦

  于是我来到迦太基

   燃烧 燃烧 燃烧 燃烧

  哦上帝你把我拔出来

(310)   哦上帝你拔

燃烧

四、死在水中

腓尼基人富勒巴斯,死了两星期,

他已忘了海鸥狂鸣,深海浪涌,

也忘了利润与亏损。

    海底的潮流

悄悄低语,捡拾他的骨头。在他漂上沉下之际

他度过了老年和青春岁月

进入了漩涡。

    不问你是基督徒还是犹太人

O you who turn the wheel and look to windward,
Consider Phlebas, who was once handsome and tall
   as you.

V. What the Thunder Said

   After the torchlight red on sweaty faces
After the frosty silence in the gardens
After the agony in stony places
The shouting and the crying
Prison and place and reverberation
Of thunder of spring over distant mountains
He who was living is now dead
We who were living are now dying
With a little patience

   Here is no water but only rock
Rock and no water and the sandy road
The road winding above among the mountains
Which are mountains of rock without water
If there were water we should stop and drink
Amongst the rock one cannot stop or think
Sweat is dry and feet are in the sand
If there were only water amongst the rock
Dead mountain mouth of carious teeth that cannot spit
Here one can neither stand nor lie nor sit

(320)　哦你转过舵轮迎风而上的人，
　　　想想富勒巴斯吧，他当年和你一样高大英俊。

五、雷声说的话

　　曾有火炬照红流汗的脸
　　曾有果园里严霜冻出的宁静
　　曾有巉岩崚嶒之处的痛苦
　　而现在，是呼喊的号叫的
　　监狱和殿堂，是春雷
　　在遥远的山那边回荡
　　那个曾经活着的人现在死了
　　我们曾经活着现在正在死去
(330)　稍有一点耐心

　　这里没有水，只有岩石
　　只有岩石，没有水，一条砂路
　　蜿蜒而上，绕进群山
　　山里只有岩石，没有水
　　假如有水，我们就会停下来喝
　　但在岩石中无法停步，无法思考
　　汗干了，脚也陷在沙里
　　要是岩石中有水就好了
　　死亡的山，满口龋齿，吐不出口水
(340)　在这儿人没法站、没法躺、没法坐

·323·

There is not even silence in the mountains
But dry sterile thunder without rain
There is not even solitude in the mountains
But red sullen faces sneer and snarl
From doors of mudcracked houses

                If there were water
  And no rock
  If there were rock
  And also water
  And water
  A spring
  A pool among the rock
  If there were the sound of water only
  Not the cicada
  And dry grass singing
  But sound of water over a rock
    Where the hermit-thrush sings in the pine trees
    Drip drop drip drop drop drop drop
    But there is no water

    Who is the third who walks always beside you?
When I count, there are only you and I together
But when I look ahead up the white road
There is always another one walking beside you
Gliding wrapt in a brown mantle, hooded

群山中甚至没有寂静
只有干枯的不生育的雷鸣，没有雨
群山中甚至找不到独处的地方
在泥墙干裂的房子门口
阴沉的红脸在冷笑，在号叫
      要是这里有水
而没有岩石
要是这里有岩石
但也有水
有水
有泉
山岩中有个水潭
要是这里有涧水的响声
而没有蝉噪
没有干枯的草在唱
只有涧水在岩石上流淌的声音
而松林中画眉的歌声
滴滴答答滴滴答答
可是实际上没有水

    那总是在你身边走的第三个人是谁？
我点数时，只有咱们两人
但当我向前看那白色的道路
我总是看到有个人走在你身边
穿着棕色大氅，戴着风帽，步履轻捷

I do not know whether a man or a woman
—But who is that on the other side of you?

   What is that sound high in the air
Murmur of maternal lamentation
Who are those hooded hordes swarming
Over endless plains, stumbling in cracked earth
Ringed by the flat horizon only   370
What is the city over the mountains
Cracks and reforms and bursts in the violet air
Falling towers
Jerusalem Athens Alexandria
Vienna London
Unreal

A woman drew her long black hair out tight
And fiddled whisper music on those strings
And bats with baby faces in the violet light
Whistled, and beat their wings   380
And crawled head downward down a blackened wall
And upside down in air were towers
Tolling reminiscent bells, that kept the hours
And voices singing out of empty cisterns and exhausted
    wells.

我不知是男人还是女人
——到底你那边是什么人?

  什么声音在高空响
是母亲悲哀的低语
那些人是谁,戴着帽兜,成群地漫过
无边的平原,在坼裂的土地上跌跌绊绊
(370) 只有地平线才是人群的边际
山那边是座什么城市
在紫色的暮气中开裂、重建、爆炸
尖塔倒倾
耶路撒冷、雅典、亚历山大
维也纳、伦敦
虚幻

一个女人揪紧她的黑长发
当作琴弦,奏出耳语般的音乐
长着孩子脸的蝙蝠在紫色的光中
(380) 飕飕地飞,拍击着翅膀
头朝下,爬进黑暗的墙根
而尖塔也在空中倒挂着
敲响引人回忆的钟,报着时辰
空水槽里、枯井里,有声音歌唱。

In this decayed hole among the mountains
In the faint moonlight, the grass is singing
Over the tumbled graves, about the chapel
There is the empty chapel, only the wind's home.
It has no windows, and the door swings,
Dry bones can harm no one.
Only a cock stood on the rooftree
Co co rico co co rico
In a flash of lightning. Then a damp gust
Bringing rain

Ganga was sunken, and the limp leaves
Waited for rain, while the black clouds
Gathered far distant, over Himavant.
The jungle crouched, humped in silence.
Then spoke the thunder
DA
Datta: what have we given?
My friend, blood shaking my heart
The awful daring of a moment's surrender
Which an age of prudence can never retract
By this, and this only, we have existed
Which is not to be found in our obituaries
Or in memories draped by the beneficent spider
Or under seals broken by the lean solicitor

　　　　在山间这个坍落的洞穴中
　　在淡淡的月光下，在殿堂四周
　　倒塌的墓上，野草在歌唱
　　这儿只有空无一物的殿堂，只有风居住。
　　没有窗子，门悬晃着，
(390)　干枯的骨头害不了人。
　　只有一只公鸡站在屋脊上
　　咯咯依咯，咯咯依咯
　　电光一闪，然后一阵潮湿的风
　　带来了雨

　　　　恒河干瘪了，萎软的叶子
　　在等着雨，而乌云
　　却在远方，在喜马万特山上聚集。
　　丛林倦起身子，静静地佝偻着。
　　然后，雷声说话了
(400)　DA
　　Datta：我们舍予过些什么？
　　我的朋友，血震撼我的心
　　瞬间的奉献要有凛然大勇
　　毕生的谨慎也无法把它收回
　　靠它，只有靠它，我们才活了下来
　　但这种奉献在我们的讣告里
　　在慈悲的蜘蛛覆盖起来的记忆里
　　在我们的空房间中被那瘦律师

In our empty rooms

DA

Dayadhvam: I have heard the key

Turn in the door once and turn once only

We think of the key, each in his prison

Thinking of the key, each confirms a prison

Only at nightfall, aetherial rumours

Revive for a moment a broken Coriolanus

DA

Damyata: The boat responded

Gaily, to the hand expert with sail and oar

The sea was calm, your heart would have
    responded

Gaily, when invited, beating obedient

To controlling hands

                    I sat upon the shore

Fishing, with the arid plain behind me

Shall I at least set my lands in order?

London Bridge is falling down falling down falling
    down

Poi s'ascose nel foco che gli affina

Quando fiam uti chelidon—O swallow swallow

Le Prince d'Aquitaine à la tour abolie

These fragments I have shored against my ruins

　　　　　　拆开的封套里，都不见提起

(410)　　DA

　　　　　　Dayadhvam：我听见钥匙

　　　　　　在门里转了一下，只转了一下

　　　　　　我们想着钥匙，每个人在各自的监狱里

　　　　　　想着钥匙，每个人守住一个监狱

　　　　　　只有在薄暮时，缥缈地传来的声音

　　　　　　才使破碎的柯莱奥兰努斯复活一阵子

　　　　　　DA

　　　　　　Damyata：在驾船行家的手里

　　　　　　船对他的驾驶欢乐地作出反应

(420)　　海多么宁静，你的心也欢乐地

　　　　　　作出反应，当你被邀请，你的心

　　　　　　会甘心在控制的手中跳动

　　　　　　　　　　　　　　我坐在岸上

　　　　　　垂钓，背后是荒瘠的平原

　　　　　　我是否至少应把这土地收拾一下？

　　　　　　伦敦桥正在塌下来塌下来塌下来

　　　　　　然后他隐入烧炼他们的火里

　　　　　　我什么时候能像燕子——哦燕子燕子

　　　　　　阿基坦王子在荒废的塔楼里

(430)　　我用这些片言只语支撑我的废墟

Why then Ile fit you. Hieronymo's mad againe.

Datta. Dayadhvam. Damyata.

Shantih shantih shantih

1922

NOTES

Not only the title, but the plan and a good deal of the incidental symbolism of the poem were suggested by Miss Jessie L. Weston's book on the Grail legend: *From Ritual to Romance*. Indeed, so deeply am I indebted, Miss Weston's book will elucidate the difficulties of the poem much better than my notes can do; and I recommend it (apart from the great interest of the book itself) to any who think such elucidation of the poem worth the trouble. To another work of anthropology I am indebted in general, one which has influenced our generation profoundly; I mean *The Golden Bough*; I have used especially the two volumes *Adonis, Attis, Osiris*. Anyone who is acquainted with these works will immediately recognise in the poem certain references to vegetation ceremonies.

I. The Burial of the Dead

Line 20 Cf. Ezekiel II, i.

23. Cf. Ecclesiastes XII, v.

31. V. *Tristan und Isolde*, I, verses 5–8.

42. Id. III, verse 24.

46. I am not familiar with the exact constitution of the Tarot pack of cards, from which I have obviously departed to suit my own convenience. The Hanged Man, a member of the traditional

好吧我就迎合你们！希罗尼莫又疯了。

舍予。同情。控制。

平安。平安。平安。

1922

艾略特自注：

这首诗的标题、构局和许多零散的象征都受杰西·L.魏斯登女士论圣杯传说的著作《从仪式到传奇》的启发。此书使我得益匪浅，实际上它比我的注释更能解释这首诗中的难点。要是有人不嫌麻烦要弄明白这首诗，我奉劝他读一读魏斯登女士的书，何况这本书本身也很有趣。总的来说，我还得益于另一本人类学著作，一本深刻地影响了我们这一代的书；我指的是《金枝》，我采用的主要是关于阿多尼斯、阿蒂斯和奥西里斯的两卷，知道这两卷著作的人会立即在诗中认出有关祈丰仪式的指代。

一、死者葬仪

20 行：参阅《以西结书》第二章第一节。

23 行：参阅《传道书》第12章第五节。

31 行：见《特利斯坦与绮索尔德》第一幕，第5至8行。

42 行：同上，第三幕，第24行。

46 行：我不太熟悉塔罗纸牌的构成，实际上我不问其实际情况，只用来派我自己的用场。这套牌中有一张"倒吊人"，我派了两个用处：在我看来，他与弗

pack, fits my purpose in two ways: because he is associated in my mind with the Hanged God of Frazer, and because I associate him with the hooded figure in the passage of the disciples to Emmaus in Part V. The Phoenician Sailor and the Merchant appear later; also the "crowds of people," and Death by Water is executed in Part IV. The Man with Three Staves (an authentic member of the Tarot pack) I associate, quite arbitrarily, with the Fisher King himself.

60. Cf. Baudelaire:

"Fourmillante cité, cité pleine de rêves,

"Où le spectre en plein jour raccroche le passant."

63. Cf. *Inferno*, III. 55–57:

"si lunga tratta

di gente, ch'io non avrei mai creduto

che morte tanta n'avesse disfatta."

64. Cf. *Inferno*, IV. 25–27:

"Quivi, secondo che per ascoltare,

"non avea pianto, ma' che di sospiri,

"che l'aura eterna facevan tremare."

68. A phenomenon which I have often noticed.

74. Cf. the Dirge in Webster's *White Devil*.

76. V. Baudelaire, Preface to *Fleurs du Mal*.

II. A Game of Chess

77. Cf. *Antony and Cleopatra*, II., ii. l. 190.

92. Laquearia. V. *Aeneid*, I, 726.

98. Sylvan scene. V. Milton, *Paradise Lost*, IV. 140.

99. V. Ovid, *Metamorphoses*, VI, Philomela.

100. Cf. Part III, l. 204.

115. Cf. Part III, l. 195.

雷泽的"绞死的神"有关系，同时又与本诗第五章耶稣门徒前往以马忤斯的路上遇到的戴风帽的人有关系。腓尼基水手与商人，以及"人群"稍后在本节出现，在第四章"死在水中"，腓尼基水手被处死。我武断地将"带三根手杖的人"（塔罗牌中确有此一张）与渔王本人联系起来。

60 行：参阅波德莱尔：

"拥挤的城市，梦魇的城市。
大白天鬼魂勾引行人。"

63 行：参阅《地狱篇》第三章第 55 至 57 行：

"人流
如此漫长，我真难相信
死神毁了那么多人。"

64 行：参阅《地狱篇》第四章第 25 至 27 行：
"在这里，听不见悲哭
的声音，只有叹息声
扰动永恒的空气。"

68 行：这是我常注意到的一个现象。

74 行：参阅韦伯斯特《白魔》中的挽歌。

76 行：见波德莱尔《恶之花》序诗。

二、一局棋

77 行：参阅《安东尼与克莉奥帕特拉》第二幕第二场第 190 行。

92 行："镶嵌天花板"，见《伊尼德》第一卷第 726 行。

98 行："山林景色"，见弥尔顿《失乐园》第四卷第 140 行。

99 行：见奥维德《变形记》第六章《费洛美拉篇》。

100 行：参阅本诗第三章第 204 行。

115 行：参阅本诗第三章第 195 行。

118. Cf. Webster: "Is the wind in that door still?"

126. Cf. Part I, l. 37, 48.

138. Cf. the game of chess in Middleton's *Women beware Women*.

III. The Fire Sermon

176. V. Spenser, *Prothalamion*.

192. Cf. *The Tempest*, I, ii.

196. Cf. Marvell, *To His Coy Mistress*.

197. Cf. Day, *Parliament of Bees*:

    "When of the sudden, listening, you shall hear,

    "A noise of horns and hunting, which shall bring

    "Actaeon to Diana in the spring,

    "Where all shall see her naked skin..."

199. I do not know the origin of the ballad from which these lines are taken: it was reported to me from Sydney, Australia.

202. V. Verlaine, *Parsifal*.

210. The currants were quoted at a price "carriage and insurance free to London"; and the Bill of Lading, etc., were to be handed to the buyer upon payment of the sight draft.

218. Tiresias, although a mere spectator and not indeed a "character", is yet the most important personage in the poem, uniting all the rest. Just as the one-eyed merchant, seller of currants, melts into the Phoenician Sailor, and the latter is not wholly distinct from Ferdinand Prince of Naples, so all the women are one woman, and the two sexes meet in Tiresias. What Tiresias *sees*, in fact, is the substance of the poem. The whole passage from Ovid is of great anthropological interest:

118行：参阅韦伯斯特的句子："风还在门里吗？"
126行：参阅本诗第一章第37行，第48行。
138行：参阅米德尔顿《女人提防女人》中的棋局。

三、火诫

176行：见斯宾塞《婚前曲》。
192行：参阅《暴风雨》第一幕第二场。
196行：参阅马弗尔《致羞怯的情妇》。
197行：参阅达伊《蜜蜂议会》：

"突然，你仔细听，就能听到，
号角和打猎的喧闹，在春天
把阿克特翁带去看狄安娜，
在那里见到她裸露的身体……"

199行：我不知道这几行诗源出于哪首民谣，有人从澳大利亚的悉尼给我抄来这首歌。

202行：见魏尔伦《帕西法尔》。

210行：这种葡萄干价格是按"运至伦敦免邮税与保险"计算的，货单在买主见单付款后交给买主。

218行：梯雷西亚斯虽然只是个旁观者，并非一个真正的"角色"，却是全诗最重要的人物，他把其他人物都联系了起来。正如那独眼商人与卖葡萄干的人一齐化成腓尼基水手，而腓尼基水手与那不勒斯王子费迪南也很难完全区分开来，同样，所有的女人也是同一个女人，而这两种性别的人在梯雷西亚斯身上融为一体。梯雷西亚斯所见到的，就是本诗的实质。奥维德的这一段话有很大的人类学价值：

> "...Cum Iunone iocos et maior vestra profecto est
> Quam, quae contingit maribus', dixisse, 'voluptas'.
> Illa negat; placuit quae sit sententia docti
> Quaerere Tiresiae: venus huic erat utraque nota.
> Nam duo magnorum viridi coeuntia silva
> Corpora serpentum baculi violaverat ictu
> Deque viro factus, mirabile, femina septem
> Egerat autumnos; octavo rursus eosdem
> Vidit et 'est vestrae si tanta potentia plagae,'
> Dixit 'ut auctoris sortem in contraria mutet,
> Nunc quoque vos feriam!' percussis anguibus isdem
> Forma prior rediit genetivaque venit imago.
> Arbiter hic igitur sumptus de lite iocosa
> Dicta Iovis firmat; gravius Saturnia iusto
> Nec pro materia fertur doluisse suique
> Iudicis aeterna damnavit lumina nocte,
> At pater omnipotens (neque enim licet inrita cuiquam
> Facta dei fecisse deo) pro lumine adempto
> Scire futura dedit poenamque levavit honore."

221. This may not appear as exact as Sappho's lines, but I had in mind the "longshore" or "dory" fisherman, who returns at nightfall.

253. V. Goldsmith, the song in *The Vicar of Wakefield*.

257. V. *The Tempest*, as above.

264. The interior of St. Magnus Martyr is to my mind one of the finest among Wren's interiors. See *The Proposed Demolition of Nineteen City Churches* (P. S. King & Son, Ltd.).

"……（朱庇特）与乔诺开起玩笑：'肯定，
你们从爱情中得到的快乐比众人多。'
她反对；他们请睿智的梯雷西亚斯
做个评判，此人了解爱情的两个方面，
因为有一次他在绿树林里遇见
正在交媾的两条巨蟒，他用棍子
打了一下，奇怪之极，他变成女人
足有七年之久；第八年他又看到
这两条蛇，他说：'既然你们具有
这样的魔力，能改变性别，那么何妨
让我再打一下！'他又打了大蛇，
由此回到了出生时的形态。
因此，他裁判两位神的争闹
说他同意朱庇特；萨都恩的女儿
勃然大怒，怒到不必要的程度，
她判处这个裁判永远处于黑夜中，
于是'全能的父'（既然没有一位神
能取消另一个神的命令）又赐给他
预言未来的本领，以这荣誉减轻处分。"

221行：这可能不太像莎孚的诗句，但我想到的是"沿岸捕鱼的"或"驾舟的"渔夫们晚上回家时的情景。

253行：见哥尔德斯密斯《威克菲尔德牧师》中的歌。

257行：见《暴风雨》，同上。

264行：在我看来，殉道堂的内部设计是雷恩的内部设计最佳作之一。见《拟议拆毁的十九个城内教堂》一书（注：金氏父子公司出版）。

266. The Song of the (three) Thames-daughters begins here. From line 292 to 306 inclusive they speak in turn. V. *Götterdämmerung*, III, i: the Rhine-daughters.

279. V. Froude, *Elizabeth*, Vol. I, ch. iv, letter of De Quadra to Philip of Spain:

> "In the afternoon we were in a barge, watching the games on the river. (The queen) was alone with Lord Robert and myself on the poop, when they began to talk nonsense, and went so far that Lord Robert at last said, as I was on the spot there was no reason why they should not be married if the queen pleased."

293. Cf. *Purgatorio*, V. 133:

> "Ricorditi di me, che son la Pia;
>
> "Siena mi fe', disfecemi Maremma."

307. V. St. Augustine's *Confessions*: "to Carthage then I came, where a cauldron of unholy loves sang all about mine ears."

308. The complete text of the Buddha's Fire Sermon (which corresponds in importance to the Sermon on the Mount) from which these words are taken, will be found translated in the late Henry Clarke Warren's *Buddhism in Translation* (Harvard Oriental Series). Mr. Warren was one of the great pioneers of Buddhist studies in the occident.

309. From St. Augustine's *Confessions* again. The collocation of these two representatives of eastern and western asceticism, as the culmination of this part of the poem, is not an accident.

V. What the Thunder Said

In the first part of Part V three themes are employed: the journey to Emmaus, the approach to the Chapel Perilous (see Miss Weston's book) and the present decay of eastern Europe.

266行：从此段开始三个泰晤士女儿之歌，从第292行至第306行她们依次说话。见《神的末日》第三幕第一景：莱茵女儿。

279行：见弗劳德《伊丽莎白》第一卷第四章，德·瓜德拉致西班牙国王腓力二世的信：

"下午我们在游艇里看河上的游戏。女王单独与罗伯特勋爵在一起，而我在船尾，他们开始讲疯话，最后罗伯特勋爵说既然有我在场，只要女王乐意，他们没有理由不结婚。"

293行：参阅《炼狱篇》第五章第133行：

"记住我，我叫拉·皮娅；

西耶纳养育了我，马雷马害了我。"

307行：见圣奥古斯丁《忏悔录》："然后我来到迦太基，一大锅不圣洁的爱在我耳边唱。"

308行：此词来自佛的《火诫》（其重要性可与《登山训众》相较），其全文见于已故亨利·克拉克·沃伦的《佛教译文集》（哈佛东方丛书）。沃伦先生是西方佛学研究的伟大先驱者之一。

309行：仍是摘自圣奥古斯丁《忏悔录》。东西方两大禁欲主义的代表作并列于此，作为本章的高潮，自非偶然。

五、雷声说的话

第五章开首部分用了三个主题：去以马忤斯的旅程，走向克殿（见魏斯登女士的书），今日东欧的糜烂。

357. This is *Turdus aonalaschkae pallasii*, the hermit-thrush which I have heard in Quebec County. Chapman says (*Handbook of Birds in Eastern North America*) "it is most at home in secluded woodland and thickety retreats... Its notes are not remarkable for variety or volume, but in purity and sweetness of tone and exquisite modulation they are unequaled." Its "water-dripping song" is justly celebrated.

360. The following lines were stimulated by the account of one of the Antarctic expeditions (I forget which, but I think one of Shackleton's): it was related that the party of explorers, at the extremity of their strength, had the constant delusion that there was *one more member* than could actually be counted.

366–76. Cf. Hermann Hesse, *Blick ins Chaos*:

"Schon ist halb Europa, schon ist zumindest der halbe Osten Europas auf dem Wege zum Chaos, fährt betrunken im heiligem Wahn am Abgrund entlang und singt dazu, singt betrunken und hymnisch wie Dmitri Karamasoff sang. Ueber diese Lieder lacht der Bürger beleidigt, der Heilige und Seher hört sie mit Tränen."

401. "Datta, dayadhvam, damyata" (Give, sympathise, control). The fable of the meaning of the Thunder is found in the *Brihadaranyaka-Upanishad*, 5, 1. A translation is found in Deussen's *Sechzig Upanishads des Veda*, p. 489.

407. Cf. Webster, *The White Devil*, V, vi:

"...they'll remarry

Ere the worm pierce your winding-sheet, ere the spider Make a thin curtain for your epitaphs."

411. Cf. *Inferno*, XXXIII, 46:

357 行：这种鸟学名为 Turdus aonalaschkae pallasii，是画眉的一种，我在魁北克听见过其鸣啼。查普曼在《美洲东北部鸟类手册》中说："这种鸟生性喜欢僻静的森林或丛林……其鸣声在变化和音量上均不突出，但音调纯朴甜美，抑扬之处十分细腻，在这方面此种鸟无与伦比。"它的"滴水歌"的确值得赞赏。

360 行：下面这几行是我读过的一次南极探险的记载（我忘了是哪一次，也许是沙克尔顿率领的那一次）而受到启发的：据报道，这一队探险家在精疲力尽时，一直出现幻觉，他们数来数去人数总是比实际的数字多一个。

366—376 行：参见赫尔曼·海塞《混乱一瞥》：

"欧洲的一半，至少东欧的一半，已经在走向混乱，在精神狂乱之中沿深渊的边界醉醺醺地驾着车，还醉醺醺地唱着歌，好像在唱圣歌，就像德米特里·卡拉马索弗一样唱着。发怒的资产阶级嘲笑这些歌；而圣人与先知则流着泪听着。"

401 行："Datta, dayadhvam, damayatta"（舍予、同情、控制）。关于雷声的寓言见圣书《奥义书》第五卷第一章，译文见多伊森《吠陀经中的六十篇奥义书》第 489 页。

407 行：参阅韦伯斯特《白魔》第五幕第六场
"……她们会重新结婚
不等蛆虫咬穿你的尸衣，不等蜘蛛
在你的墓志铭上织一层网。"

411 行：参阅《地狱篇》第 33 章第 46 行：

"ed io sentii chiavar l'uscio di sotto

all'orribile torre."

Also F. H. Bradley, *Appearance and Reality*, p. 346.

"My external sensations are no less private to myself than are my thoughts or my feelings. In either case my experience falls within my own circle, a circle closed on the outside; and, with all its elements alike, every sphere is opaque to the others which surround it… In brief, regarded as an existence which appears in a soul, the whole world for each is peculiar and private to that soul."

424. V. Weston, *From Ritual to Romance*; chapter on the Fisher King.

427. V. *Purgatorio*, XXVI, 148.

"'Ara vos prec, per aquella valor

'que vos guida al som de l'escalina,

'sovegna vos a temps de ma dolor.'

Poi s'ascose nel foco che gli affina."

428. V. *Pervigilium Veneris*. Cf. Philomela in Parts II and III.

429. V. Gerard de Nerval, Sonnet *El Desdichado*.

431. V. Kyd's *Spanish Tragedy*.

433. Shantih. Repeated as here, a formal ending to an Upanishad. "The Peace which passeth understanding" a feeble translation of the content of this word.

"我听见下面这恐怖的塔

被锁上了门。"

另外参见 F. H. 布拉得雷《表象与实在》第 346 页：

"我的外部感觉也和我的思想和感情一样，完全属于我个人。无论在哪一方面，我的经验只落在我自己的领域中，这领域是对外封闭的。而这领域的各个圈子互相隔绝，因为他们的成分相同……简单地说，每个人的全部世界，作为出现于灵魂中的一种存在，对这灵魂来说是特殊的、独有的。"

424 行：见魏斯登《从仪式到传奇》有关渔王的一章。

427 行：见《炼狱篇》第 26 章第 148 节："因此我凭着把你

领上楼梯顶的美德请求你，

在适当时候想起我的痛苦，

然后他又潜入烧炼他们的火里。"

428 行：见《维纳斯的无眠之夜》。参见本诗第二章和第三章费洛美拉的故事。

429 行：见热拉尔·德·内瓦尔的十四行诗《被剥夺继承权的人》。

431 行：见基德《西班牙悲剧》。

433 行："平安"在此重复，这是某一部《奥义书》的正式结尾，此词的意义大略可译成"超出一切理解的安宁"。

The Hollow Men

Mistah Kurtz—he dead.

A penny for the Old Guy

I

We are the hollow men
We are the stuffed men
Leaning together
Headpiece filled with straw. Alas!
Our dried voices, when
We whisper together
Are quiet and meaningless
As wind in dry grass
Or rats' feet over broken glass
In our dry cellar

Shape without form, shade without colour,
Paralysed force, gesture without motion;

Those who have crossed
With direct eyes, to death's other Kingdom

空心人

库尔兹先生——他死了[1]
给老盖伊一文钱吧[2]

一

我们是空心人

我们是填塞起来的人

靠在一起

脑袋瓜装一包草。唉!

当我们窃窃私语

我们干涩的嗓音

平静而无意义

像风吹干草

或是干燥的地窖里

耗子在碎玻璃上跑

有形无式,有影无色,

瘫痪的力量,不动的姿势;

那些眼光直朝前地

跨进死亡的另一个国土的人

---

1 库尔兹是康拉德著名中篇小说《黑暗的心脏》的主人公,他在小说的结尾死去。
2 盖伊指英国历史上著名的火药爆炸案主角盖伊·福克斯(Guy Fawkes),英国有风俗每年的11月5日会焚烧盖伊·福克斯纸像,而孩子们假装乞讨,喊着这句话。

Remember us—if at all—not as lost
Violent souls, but only
As the hollow men
The stuffed men.

II

Eyes I dare not meet in dreams
In death's dream kingdom
These do not appear:
There, the eyes are
Sunlight on a broken column
There, is a tree swinging
And voices are
In the wind's singing
More distant and more solemn
Than a fading star.

Let me be no nearer
In death's dream kingdom
Let me also wear
Such deliberate disguises
Rat's coat, crowskin, crossed staves
In a field
Behaving as the wind behaves
No nearer—

万一——记得我们——不要像迷路的

狂暴的灵魂,而仅仅

是空心人

填塞起来的人。

二

在梦中,在死亡的梦幻之国

我不敢遇见的眼睛

并没有出现:

在那里,眼睛只是

破碎的圆柱上的阳光

在那里,是摇曳的树

而嗓音混合在

风的歌声中

比渐渐暗淡的星

更加遥远,更加庄严。

让我别再走近

死神的梦幻之国

让我也穿起

这些特意的伪装

老鼠外套,乌鸦皮,交叉的棍子

在田野里

跟风一样行动

不能再走近——

Not that final meeting
In the twilight kingdom

III

This is the dead land
This is the cactus land
Here the stone images
Are raised, here they receive
The supplication of a dead man's hand
Under the twinkle of a fading star.

Is it like this
In death's other kingdom
Waking alone
At the hour when we are
Trembling with tenderness
Lips that would kiss
Form prayers to broken stone.

IV

The eyes are not here
There are no eyes here
In this valley of dying stars
In this hollow valley
This broken jaw of our lost kingdoms

不是在暮光世界

那最后的相会

三

这是死去的土地

这是仙人掌的土地

在这里竖立着

石头雕像,在渐渐暗淡的

星光之中,他们接受

死人手臂的哀求。

就像这样

在死亡的另一个国度

独自醒来时

正值我们

因柔情而战栗

那准备接吻的双唇

说出了对破碎石头的祈祷。

四

眼睛不在这里

眼睛不在这里

这星星死亡的山谷

这空虚的山谷

我们失去了的天国的破牙床

In this last of meeting places

We grope together

And avoid speech

Gathered on this beach of the tumid river

Sightless, unless

The eyes reappear

As the perpetual star

Multifoliate rose

Of death's twilight kingdom

The hope only

Of empty men.

V

Here we go round the prickly pear
Prickly pear, prickly pear
Here we go round the prickly pear
At five o'clock in the morning.

Between the idea

And the reality

Between the motion

在这最后一个相会地点

我们摸索到一齐

一言不发

会集在这涨水的河流岸边

一无所见,除非

眼睛重新出现

好像永恒的星辰

好像死亡的晦冥之国里

那复瓣的玫瑰

那是空心人的

唯一希冀。

五

在这里我们围绕着多刺的梨

多刺的梨,多刺的梨

在这里我们围绕着多刺的梨

在大清早五点。[1]

就在思想

和现实之间

就在行动

---

[1] "多刺的梨"指仙人掌,荒漠中唯一的植物,这段诗是戏仿一首儿歌:"我们围着桑树跳舞,在冰冷的早上。"(Here we go round the mulberry bush, On a cold and frosty morning.)

And the act

Falls the Shadow

> *For Thine is the Kingdom*

Between the conception

And creation

Between the emotion

And the response

Falls the Shadow

> *Life is very long*

Between the desire

And the spasm

Between the potency

And the existence

Between the essence

And the descent

Falls the Shadow

> *For Thine is the Kingdom*

For Thine is

Life is

For Thine is the

和动作之间

落下了影子

   因为天国属于你

就在概念

和创造之间

就在情绪

和反应之间

落下了影子

   生命可真长

就在愿望

和痉挛之间

就在潜力

和存在之间

就在本质

和后果之间

落下了影子

   因为天国属于你

因为是你的

生命是

因为是你的这

This is the way the world ends
This is the way the world ends
This is the way the world ends
Not with a bang but a whimper.

1925

Journey of the Magi

'A cold coming we had of it,
Just the worst time of the year
For a journey, and such a long journey:
The ways deep and the weather sharp,
The very dead of winter.'
And the camels galled, sore-footed, refractory,
Lying down in the melting snow.
There were times we regretted
The summer palaces on slopes, the terraces,
And the silken girls bringing sherbet.
Then the camel men cursing and grumbling
And running away, and wanting their liquor and
    women,
And the night-fires going out, and the lack of shelters,

世界正如此告终

世界正如此告终

世界正如此告终

没有一声轰隆[1]，只剩一声唏嘘。

1925

三贤哲的旅程[2]

"这一路可真冷

正是一年中最不便

旅行之时，而且旅程这么长：

道路泥泞，冬气凛冽，

正是岁晚寒深。"

那些骆驼皮肉擦伤，脚掌疼痛，倔强难制，

躺倒在融化的雪中。

有时我们真想念

山坡上的夏宫，那凉台，

穿丝绸衣服的女郎送来冰果汁。

然而赶骆驼的人咒骂着，抱怨着，

离队逃走，去寻找酒和女人，

篝火也灭了，无处蔽身，

城市敌视外人，小镇板起面孔

---

1 暗指火药爆炸案，意思是现代人无此魄力。
2 据《新约·马太福音》第二章，耶稣降生时，有三贤哲自东方来朝见。

And the cities hostile and the towns unfriendly
And the villages dirty and charging high prices:
A hard time we had of it.
At the end we preferred to travel all night,
Sleeping in snatches,
With the voices singing in our ears, saying
That this was all folly.

Then at dawn we came down to a temperate valley,
Wet, below the snow line, smelling of vegetation;
With a running stream and a water-mill beating the darkness,
And three trees on the low sky,
And an old white horse galloped away in the meadow.
Then we came to a tavern with vine-leaves over the lintel,
Six hands at an open door dicing for pieces of silver,
And feet kicking the empty wine-skins.
But there was no information, and so we continued
And arrived at evening, not a moment too soon
Finding the place; it was (you may say) satisfactory.

All this was a long time ago, I remember,
And I would do it again, but set down
This set down
This: were we lead all that way for
Birth or Death? There was a Birth, certainly,

村庄肮脏不堪,又漫天要价:

这一路真够受的。

最后我们情愿整夜赶路

断断续续打盹,

有声音在耳边唱,说是

这实在是一桩蠢事。

黎明时我们走进一个温暖的山谷

雪线以下气候湿润,充满花草的芬芳,

涧水涓涓,水磨捶打着黑暗

低垂的夜空中有三棵树,

一匹白色的老马奔过草地。

然后我们走到一个旅店,葡萄叶长满窗楣,

六个汉子坐在开着的门前,掷骰赌钱,

脚踢着倒空的酒囊。

问不出什么情况,我们再往前走,

晚上才到达,正赶上,

找到这里;可以说总算不错。

这都是很久前的事了,我记得,

我愿意重走一次,但先记下来,

先把这些记下来:

我们一路而来,是为了

诞生还是死亡?曾经有过诞生,当然,

We had evidence and no doubt. I have seen birth and
    death,
But had thought they were different; this Birth was
Hard and bitter agony for us, like Death, our death.
We returned to our places, these Kingdoms,
But no longer at ease here, in the old dispensation,
With an alien people clutching their gods.
I should be glad of another death.

1927

我们有证据，无可怀疑。我见过诞生和死亡，
但以前总认为它们不相像；而这次诞生
刀剜肺腑地痛，像死，像我们自己死一样。
我们回到家乡，回到这些王国，
但心境再难安宁，全套的古旧习俗，
已成陌路的人们死守着他们的神祇。
我情愿再死一次。

1927

华莱斯·斯蒂文斯
(Wallace Stevens, 1879-1955)

斯蒂文斯常被称为"诗人的诗人"或"批评家的诗人"。他不是一夜成名,1914年他开始在《诗刊》上发表诗作时年龄已不小,1923年他的第一本诗集《风琴》一开始只售出100本,直到20世纪四五十年代这本诗集才为人所知,被公认为美国现代诗歌的杰作。他使人炫目的风格在这本诗集中已充分展现。此后,他在作品哲理上的开掘更为深入。

斯蒂文斯的诗以意义难解著称,他用词突兀、色彩浓丽、奇瑰诡谲,连字面意义有时都在可解不可解之间。但是他的许多诗作围绕着一个主题:艺术想象力与现实的关系,即人的诗意想象力如何观照并改变现实。在这种思索中,他落入许多美国现代派诗人共有的唯心主义,认为世界以及经验都不可避免地混乱不堪,只有艺术(即想象的力量)能赋予它以秩序和形态。

斯蒂文斯本人的职业是律师,自20世纪30年代起就在一家保险公司任经理,直到逝世。这职业与他的诗人生涯实在是出奇地不相称。

20世纪50年代初,斯蒂文斯接连得到美国三大诗歌奖的肯定:波林根奖(1949年)、全国图书奖(1951年、1955年)、普利策奖(1955年)。而在他逝世后,他的声誉反而越来越高,不少年轻诗人以他的作品为师,关于他的评论著作也日益增多,使他成为美国现代诗歌史上与庞德、艾略特、威廉斯等人比肩的最重要的诗人之一。

Domination of Black

At night, by the fire,

The colors of the bushes

And of the fallen leaves,

Repeating themselves,

Turned in the room,

Like the leaves themselves

Turning in the wind.

Yes: but the color of the heavy hemlocks

Came striding.

And I remembered the cry of the peacocks.

The colors of their tails

Were like the leaves themselves

Turning in the wind,

In the twilight wind.

They swept over the room,

Just as they flew from the boughs of the hemlocks

Down to the ground.

I heard them cry—the peacocks.

Was it a cry against the twilight

Or against the leaves themselves

Turning in the wind,

Turning as the flames

黑色的统治

在夜里,在炉火边,
树丛的各种色彩,
落叶的各种色调,
重复再现,
在房间里翻卷,
就像树叶本身
在风中翻卷
是啊:浓密的铁杉树的色彩
大步走来。
我想起了孔雀的叫喊。

孔雀尾翎的各种色彩
也像这树叶
翻卷,在风中,
在黄昏的风中。
色彩扫过房间,
就像孔雀从铁杉树上
飞落地面。
我听到它们呼喊——这些孔雀
那呼喊是抗议暮色,
还是抗议树叶
在风中翻卷?
翻卷,好像火焰

Turned in the fire,

Turning as the tails of the peacocks

Turned in the loud fire,

Loud as the hemlocks

Full of the cry of the peacocks?

Or was it a cry against the hemlocks?

Out of the window,

I saw how the planets gathered

Like the leaves themselves

Turning in the wind.

I saw how the night came,

Came striding like the color of the heavy hemlocks

I felt afraid.

And I remembered the cry of the peacocks.

1923

The Snow Man

One must have a mind of winter

To regard the frost and the boughs

Of the pine-trees crusted with snow;

在燃烧时翻卷,

翻卷,好像孔雀尾翎

在喧闹的火焰中翻卷,

高声地,好像铁杉树里

充满了孔雀的叫喊?

要不这呼喊是在抗议铁杉?

从窗口望出去,

我看到行星聚拢,

就好像树叶

在风中翻卷。

我看到黑夜来临

大步走来,像浓密的铁杉的颜色,

我感到害怕,

我记起了孔雀的叫喊。

1923

雪中人

人须有冬天的心境,

才能看霜,看雪

裹满了松树的枝丫;

And have been cold a long time
To behold the junipers shagged with ice,
The spruces rough in the distant glitter

Of the January sun; and not to think
Of any misery in the sound of the wind,
In the sound of a few leaves,

Which is the sound of the land
Full of the same wind
That is blowing in the same bare place

For the listener, who listens in the snow,
And, nothing himself, beholds
Nothing that is not there and the nothing that is.

1923

Valley Candle

My candle burned alone in an immense valley.
Beams of the huge night converged upon it,
Until the wind blew.
The beams of the huge night

人须自己长期挨冻,

才能看杜松挂满冰针

而针枞在遥远的

正月阳光中显得粗糙;他才能

不去想在风声中,在几张残叶

的声音中,有多少凄苦,

这风声是大地的声音

大地充满同样的风

在同样荒芜的地方

为雪地里的聆听者吹送,

他自己是乌有,因此看到

不存在的乌有和存在的乌有。

1923

山谷中的蜡烛

无边的山谷中只有我的蜡烛燃烧。

巨大的夜所有的光线汇集到它上面,

直到风吹来。

巨大的夜的光线

Converged upon its image,

Until the wind blew.

1923

The Emperor of Ice-cream

Call the roller of big cigars,

The muscular one, and bid him whip

In kitchen cups concupiscent curds.

Let the wenches dawdle in such dress

As they are used to wear, and let the boys

Bring flowers in last month's newspapers.

Let be be finale of seem.

The only emperor is the emperor of ice-cream.

Take from the dresser of deal.

Lacking the three glass knobs, that sheet

On which she embroidered fantails once

And spread it so as to cover her face.

If her horny feet protrude, they come

To show how cold she is, and dumb.

汇集到它的形象上,

直到风吹来。

1923

冰淇淋皇帝[1]

叫一下那个卷大雪茄的人,

那肌肉发达的汉子,告诉他

到厨房里打一杯色情的冰淇淋。

让娘儿们穿着平时的衣服

过来闲逛,让那些男孩

带着花束,裹着上个月的报纸。

让"似乎"最后变成"就是"。

唯一的皇帝是冰淇淋皇帝。

松木柜掉了三个玻璃把手,

请从里面取出那条

她绣了扇尾鸽的被单

铺开,盖没她的脸。

她粗硬的脚伸出,那正是

在表示她已全身冰冷,不会说话。

---

[1] 斯蒂文斯在一封信中说:"此诗主题当然不是讲冰淇淋,而是说存在与貌似存在是有区别的。"

Let the lamp affix its beam.

The only emperor is the emperor of ice-cream.

1923

Anecdote of the Jar

I placed a jar in Tennessee,
And round it was, upon a hill.
It made the slovenly wilderness
Surround that hill.

The wilderness rose up to it,
And sprawled around, no longer wild.
The jar was round upon the ground
And tall and of a port in air.

It took dominion everywhere.
The jar was gray and bare.
It did not give of bird or bush,
Like nothing else in Tennessee.

1923

让灯把光线贴上去。

唯一的皇帝是冰淇淋皇帝。

1923

坛子的轶事[1]

我把一只坛放在田纳西,

它是圆的,置在山巅。

它使凌乱的荒野

围着山峰排列。

于是荒野向坛子涌起,

匍匐在四周,再不荒莽。

坛子圆圆地置在地上

高高屹立,巍峨庄严。

它君临着四面八方。

坛是灰色的,未施彩妆。

它无法产生鸟或树丛,

不像田纳西别的事物。

1923

---

1 "坛"是艺术想象力的象征,斯蒂文斯认为艺术不能产生"鸟或树丛"那样的现实事物,却能赋予混乱的世界以一种秩序。

Peter Quince at the Clavier

I

Just as my fingers on these keys
Make music, so the self-same sounds
On my spirit make a music, too.

Music is feeling, then, not sound;
And thus it is that what I feel,
Here in this room, desiring you,

Thinking of your blue-shadowed silk,
Is music. It is like the strain
Waked in the elders by Susanna;

Of a green evening, clear and warm,
She bathed in her still garden, while
The red-eyed elders, watching, felt

The basses of their beings throb

彼得·昆士弹琴[1]

一

正当我的手指在键上
弹出音乐,这些声音
在我心中也形成音乐。

因此音乐是感觉,不是声音;
因此,此时此地,
在这房间里,我渴望你,

想念你蓝幽幽的绸衣,
就是音乐。它正如苏珊娜[2]
在长者们心中唤起的曲调;

绿色的夜晚,清澈,温暖,
她在宁静的花园沐浴,这时
眼睛发红的长者看着,感到

他们生命的低音区震荡出

---

[1] 彼得·昆士是莎士比亚《仲夏夜之梦》中的一个人物,他邀集一批工匠伙伴排演一场戏。在这首诗中,彼得·昆士作为主人公以第一人称弹奏出一个故事。

[2] 苏珊娜的故事,见《旧约·但以理书》。巴比伦一富商之妻苏珊娜在庭中沐浴,两个年长歹徒在树丛后窥视,顿起淫心,欲行非礼。苏珊娜不从,急呼求救,而二长者也喊叫,说苏珊娜与人通奸。法庭判苏珊娜死刑,而先知但以理要求复审,并分别审问二长者,发现两人证词互不相符。因此苏珊娜无罪获释,而二长者被判死刑。

In witching chords, and their thin blood
Pulse pizzicati of Hosanna.

II

In the green water, clear and warm,
Susanna lay.
She searched
The touch of springs,
And found
Concealed imaginings.
She sighed,
For so much melody.

Upon the bank, she stood
In the cool
Of spent emotions.
She felt, among the leaves,
The dew
Of old devotions.

She walked upon the grass,
Still quavering.
The winds were like her maids,
On timid feet,
Fetching her woven scarves,

销魂的和弦,而稀薄的血,
蹦跳着,拨奏赞美之声。

二

绿色的水,清澈,温暖,
苏珊娜躺在水里。
她寻求
春天的抚摸,
只找到
隐藏的想象。
她叹息
因为旋律太多。

她站到岸上
激情消退
心绪安宁。
纷纷落叶中,她感到
往昔的忠诚
如露滴。

她在草上走,
依然在打颤。
风像她的使女
步履羞怯地跟着,
给她取来

Yet wavering.

A breath upon her hand
Muted the night.
She turned—
A cymbal crashed,
And roaring horns.

III

Soon, with a noise like tambourines,
Came her attendant Byzantines.

They wondered why Susanna cried
Against the elders by her side;

And as they whispered, the refrain
Was like a willow swept by rain.

Anon, their lamps' uplifted flame
Revealed Susanna and her shame.

And then, the simpering Byzantines
Fled, with a noise like tambourines.

还在摇摆的头巾。

一口气吹在她手上
使夜悄然无声。
她转过身——
一声铙钹敲响,
号角齐鸣。

三

很快,伴着手鼓的敲击,
来了她的拜占庭婢女。

她们不明白为什么
苏珊娜对长者呵斥;

她们低语,那迭句
像打着柳叶的雨。

不久,她们的灯焰升起,
照亮了苏珊娜和她的羞耻。

于是痴笑的拜占庭少女
逃了,伴着手鼓的敲击。

IV

Beauty is momentary in the mind—
The fitful tracing of a portal;
But in the flesh it is immortal.

The body dies; the body's beauty lives.
So evenings die, in their green going,
A wave, interminably flowing.
So gardens die, their meek breath scenting
The cowl of winter, done repenting.
So maidens die, to the auroral
Celebration of a maiden's choral.

Susanna's music touched the bawdy strings
Of those white elders; but, escaping,
Left only Death's ironic scraping.
Now, in its immortality, it plays
On the clear viol of her memory,
And makes a constant sacrament of praise.

1923

四

美在头脑中转瞬即逝——
像大门时开时合；
但是在肉体中它却不朽。

肉体死亡；肉体的美永存。
正如晚景消失，绿莹莹地出走，
而波浪却不停地流。
正如花园荒芜，而柔弱的呼吸
察觉到冬天的僧帽，完成忏悔。
正如姑娘死去，而少女的合唱
欢庆来临的曙光。

苏珊娜的音乐拨响了
这些白发长者淫心的弦；但她逃跑
只留下死神嘲弄的刮搔。
现在，在永恒中，音乐表演
记着她的六弦琴，
做出永远不变的赞美诺言。

1923

Thirteen Ways of Looking at a Blackbird

I

Among twenty snowy mountains,
The only moving thing
Was the eye of the blackbird.

II

I was of three minds,
Like a tree
In which there are three blackbirds.

III

The blackbird whirled in the autumn winds.
It was a small part of the pantomime.

IV

A man and a woman
Are one.
A man and a woman and a blackbird
Are one.

看黑鸟的十三种方式[1]

一

二十座雪山之中

只有一个东西在动,

那是黑鸟的眼睛。

二

我有三个心灵,

好像一棵树

有三只黑鸟栖息。

三

黑鸟回翔在秋风中。

它是哑剧的一小部分。

四

一个男人和一个女人

是一回事。

一个男人和一个女人和一只黑鸟

是一回事。

---

[1] "黑鸟"在这里象征诗的想象力,13首短诗分别阐述想象力在诗歌创作中如何发挥作用。黑鸟(blackbird),应当译为"乌鸫",是一种画眉,但在这里诗人调动了"鸟"这一名词中的色感,对于鸟本身的特征并不关注,因此,试译为"黑鸟"。

V

I do not know which to prefer,
The beauty of inflections
Or the beauty of innuendoes,
The blackbird whistling
Or just after.

VI

Icicles filled the long window
With barbaric glass.
The shadow of the blackbird
Crossed it, to and fro.
The mood
Traced in the shadow
An indecipherable cause.

VII

O thin men of Haddam,
Why do you imagine golden birds?
Do you not see how the blackbird
Walks around the feet
Of the women about you?

五

我不知道该挑哪一个,

是词形变化之美,

还是词义暗示之美,

是黑鸟啼啭之时,

还是鸟鸣乍停之际。

六

冰串儿填满了

玻璃粗蛮的长窗。

黑鸟的身影

掠过窗子,来来去去。

影子描画出

情绪

原因很难解释。

七

哦哈达姆[1]瘦弱的人,

你为什么幻想金鸟?

你没见到黑鸟

在你周围女人的

脚下跳来跳去?

---

1 美国康涅狄格州一滨海小城。斯蒂文斯自己说这地名是任意选的。

VIII

I know noble accents

And lucid, inescapable rhythms;

But I know, too,

That the blackbird is involved

In what I know.

IX

When the blackbird flew out of sight,

It marked the edge

Of one of many circles.

X

At the sight of blackbirds

Flying in a green light,

Even the bawds of euphony

Would cry out sharply.

XI

He rode over Connecticut

In a glass coach.

Once, a fear pierced him,

In that he mistook

八

我懂得高贵的声调

和澄澈的,无法回避的节奏;

但我也知道,

我懂得的事情

都跟黑鸟有关。

九

当黑鸟远飞高翔,渺无踪影,

它画出了

许多圆圈中某一个的边界。

十

当我们见到黑鸟

在绿光中疾飞,

哪怕是买卖音韵的人[1]

也会惊叫起来。

十一

有人坐玻璃马车

穿过康涅狄格州,

一次,他惊恐万分,

因为他

---

[1] 买卖音韵的人,指光注意格律形式的学院派诗人。这节诗是说真正的诗意所带来的感觉能迫使他们改变写作风格。

The shadow of his equipage

For blackbirds.

XII

The river is moving.

The blackbird must be flying.

XIII

It was evening all afternoon.

It was snowing

And it was going to snow.

The blackbird sat

In the cedar-limbs.

1923

The Death of a Soldier

Life contracts and death is expected,

As in season of autumn.

The soldier falls.

He does not become a three-days' personage.

把马车的影子
当作了黑鸟。

十二
大河动荡,
黑鸟准是在飞。

十三
整个下午都如傍晚,
飞雪不断,
还将下雪。
黑鸟栖在
杉树的枝头。

1923

士兵之死

生命收缩,死已可期,
就像在秋天,
这士兵倒下。

他没有变成轰动三天的人物。

Imposing his separation,

Calling for pomp.

Death is absolute and without memorial,

As in a season of autumn,

When the wind stops,

When the wind stops and, over the heavens,

The clouds go, nevertheless,

In their direction.

1923

Dance of the Macabre Mice

In the land of turkeys in turkey weather

At the base of the statue, we go round and round.

What a beautiful history, beautiful surprise!

Monsieur is on horseback. The horse is covered with mice.

This dance has no name. It is a hungry dance.

We dance it out to the tip of Monsieur's sword,

Reading the lordly language of the inscription,

把告别强加于人,
搞得泱泱壮观。

死是绝对的,没有怀念,
就像在秋天,
金风骤停。

金风骤停,但在天上,
白云依然
走自己的路。

1923

恐怖的鼠之舞

在火鸡的国土,在火鸡的天气
围着雕像的基座我们舞了又舞。
多漂亮的历史,多漂亮的奇迹!
英雄骑在马上,马上爬满老鼠。

这舞没有名字,它是饥饿之舞。
我们笔直舞到英雄的剑尖,
我们读着题铭的庄严词句,

Which is like zithers and tambourines combined:

The Founder of the State. Whoever founded
A state that was free, in the dead of winter, from
   mice?
What a beautiful tableau tinted and towering,
The arm of bronze outstretched against all evil!

1935

The Man with the Blue Guitar (Excerpts)

I

The man bent over his guitar,
A shearsman of sorts. The day was green.

They said, "You have a blue guitar,
You do not play things as they are."

The man replied, "Things as they are
Are changed upon the blue guitar."

读来就像筝琴与手鼓合奏:

建国元勋。有谁建立过一个
能在严冬时免于鼠害的国家?
好个美景,层层上色,高高耸立,
青铜的手臂伸出打击一切罪恶!

1935

弹蓝色吉他的人(选段)[1]

一

那人俯身在他的吉他上
样子像裁缝。天色正发绿。

他们说:"你有把蓝色吉他,
但你没弹出如实的真情。"

这人回答说:"如实的真情,
也在这蓝吉他上发生变更。"

---

1 《弹蓝色吉他的人》共33节,题意取自毕加索"蓝色时期"所绘的一幅《盲眼的弹吉他的人》(1903年)。斯蒂文斯后来解释说:"我想写的是四件事:1. 现实;2. 想象;3. 两者的关系;4. 主要是我对这三者的态度。"

And they said then, "But play, you must,
A tune beyond us, yet ourselves,

A tune upon the blue guitar
Of things exactly as they are."

II

I cannot bring a world quite round,
Although I patch it as I can.

I sing a hero's head, large eye
And bearded bronze, but not a man,

Although I patch him as I can
And reach through him almost to man.

If to serenade almost to man
Is to miss, by that, things as they are,

Say it is the serenade
Of a man that plays a blue guitar.

XXVI

The world washed in his imagination,
The world was a shore, whether sound or form

因此他们说:"你必须弹个,
既超越又实写我们的曲子,

在蓝吉他上弹出个曲子
要恰如事物其分的样子。"

二

我没法把一个世界弄得滚圆,
虽然我尽所能贴贴补补。

我歌唱英雄的头,巨大的眼,
长胡子的铜像,但唱不出人。

虽然我尽我所能贴贴补补,
而且靠它差点儿够着了人。

要是够着小夜曲就是够着人,
那就是搞错了事物的真相。

只能说那是人的小夜曲
在俯身弹奏蓝色的吉他。

二十六

世界在他的想象中洗刷,
世界是岸,不管声音、形式

Or light, the relic of farewells,
Rock, of valedictory echoings,

To which his imagination returned,
From which it sped, a bar in space,

Sand heaped in the clouds, giant that fought
Against the murderous alphabet:

The swarm of thoughts, the swarm of dreams
Of inaccessible Utopia.

A mountainous music always seemed
To be falling and to be passing away.

1937

Dry Loaf

It is equal to living in a tragic land
To live in a tragic time.
Regard now the sloping, the mountainous rocks
And the river that batters its way over stones,
Regard the hovels of those that live in this land.

还是光,告别的遗迹,
岩石,辞行的回声,

他的想象总是回溯这些东西,
又从它们驰开,像光射入空间,

像沙堆在云中,像巨人
在与凶残的字母搏斗:

麇集的世界,麇集的梦,
梦见一个不可企及的乌托邦。

大山一般的音乐似乎
在不断倒下,在消失。

1937

干面包

生活在一个悲剧的土地上
正像生活在一个悲剧的时代。
现在请看这缓缓倾斜的山岩,
从石头中打出一条路的江河,
看这土地上生活的人住的茅舍。

That was what I painted behind the loaf,
The rocks not even touched by snow,
The pines along the river and the dry men blown
Brown as the bread, thinking of birds
Flying from burning countries and brown sand shores.

Birds that came like dirty water in waves
Flowing above the rocks, flowing over the sky,
As if the sky was a current that bore them along,
Spreading them as waves spread flat on the shore,
One after another washing the mountains bare.

It was the battering of drums I heard.
It was hunger, it was the hungry that cried
And the waves, the waves were soldiers moving,
Marching and marching in a tragic time
Below me, on the asphalt, under the trees.

It was soldiers went marching over the rocks
And still the birds came, came in watery flocks,
Because it was spring and the birds had to come.
No doubt that soldiers had to be marching
And that drums had to be rolling, rolling, rolling.

1942

这就是我在面包后面画的景色,
从来没沾过飞雪的巍巍山岩,
沿河的松林,风吹干的人
面包一般棕黄,思念着那些
来自火焰之国和棕色沙岸的鸟。

飞鸟来到,像波澜层层的污水,
从岩石上漫过,从天空中漫过,
似乎天空是条巨流把他们裹起,
又洒开,就如波浪漫洒在海岸,
后浪接前浪,把山脉洗得光秃。

而我听到的却是战鼓在猛击。
是饥饿,是饥饿的人们在呼喊,
这波浪,这波浪是士兵在前进,
行进,行进在一个悲剧的时代
在窗下,柏油路上,树木下面。

这是士兵在山岩上面行进,
而鸟仍像水波般一群群飞来。
因为这是春天,是鸟飞来之时,
无可怀疑士兵们也得不断行进,
而鼓声必须不断轰鸣,轰鸣,轰鸣。

1942

Of Modern Poetry

The poem of the mind in the act of finding
What will suffice. It has not always had
To find: the scene was set; it repeated what
Was in the script.
                    Then the theatre was changed
To something else. Its past was a souvenir.

It has to be living, to learn the speech of the place.
It has to face the men of the time and to meet
The women of the time. It has to think about war
And it has to find what will suffice. It has
To construct a new stage. It has to be on that stage,
And, like an insatiable actor, slowly and
With meditation, speak words that in the ear,
In the delicatest ear of the mind, repeat,
Exactly, that which it wants to hear, at the sound
Of which, an invisible audience listens,
Not to the play, but to itself, expressed
In an emotion as of two people, as of two
Emotions becoming one. The actor is
A metaphysician in the dark, twanging
An instrument, twanging a wiry string that gives

论现代诗歌

这诗写思维在行动中寻找
令人满足的东西。不一定每次
都找到：布景已搭好；它重复
写好的脚本。
    然后剧院改演
一出新戏。过去的只剩回忆。

诗必须活着，学会当地的话，
它得面对这时代的男人，会见
这时代的女人。它也得想战争，
得找出何物令人满意。它必须
搭一个新台。他必须站在台上，
像个永不满足的演员，缓慢地
沉思地，咏出台词，在那耳朵，
在思维的最敏感的耳朵中恰好
重复它正想听的东西，这声音
一群看不见的观众正在倾听，
不是听戏，而是听自己被表现，
情绪上好像是两个人，两种
情绪结合成一体。演员应是
黑暗中的玄学家，拨动他的
乐器，拨动一根金属丝的弦，

Sounds passing through sudden rightnesses, wholly
Containing the mind, below which it cannot descend,
Beyond which it has no will to rise.
             It must
Be the finding of a satisfaction, and may
Be of a man skating, a woman dancing, a woman
Combing. The poem of the act of the mind.

                                                    1942

The Motive for Metaphor

You like it under the trees in autumn,
Because everything is half dead.
The wind moves like a cripple among the leaves
And repeats words without meaning.

In the same way, you were happy in spring,
With the half colors of quarter-things,
The slightly brighter sky, the melting clouds,
The single bird, the obscure moon—

The obscure moon lighting an obscure world
Of things that would never be quite expressed,

琴声穿越突然的准确性,整个
包裹了思想,不能低于这水平
也没有超越它的愿望。
　　它必须
找到令人满意的东西,可以是
一个男人滑冰,一个女人跳舞,
或者梳头。思维在行动中的诗。

1942

比喻的动机

你喜欢在秋天的树下,
因为一切都半死不活。
风在树叶中走,像跛子,
重复那些没意义的词。

同样原因,春天你很幸福,
四下分的东西,两半的颜色,
稍微亮些的天,消融的云,
孤独的鸟,幽暗的月亮——

幽暗的月亮,照着幽暗世界,
充满了无法表达的事物。

Where you yourself were not quite yourself,
And did not want nor have to be,

Desiring the exhilarations of changes:
The motive for metaphor, shrinking from
The weight of primary noon,
The A B C of being,

The ruddy temper, the hammer
Of red and blue, the hard sound—
Steel against intimation—the sharp flash,
The vital, arrogant, fatal, dominant X.

1947

Notes Toward a Supreme Fiction (Excerpts)

IV

Two things of opposite natures seem to depend
On one another, as a man depends
On a woman, day on night, the imagined

在那儿你永远没法自在,

你不想自在,你也不必,

企望变化的那种兴奋:

就是比喻的动机,它躲避

那最初的正午的压力,

躲避存在的 A、B、C。

殷红的淬火,红的蓝的

锤子,沉重的声音——

钢的打击暗示——刺眼的火光,

那重要、傲慢、致命、主宰的 X。[1]

1947

最高虚构笔记(选段)[2]

四

两个本质相反的东西似乎

互相依靠对方,就像男人

依靠女人,日靠夜,想象

---

[1] 可参考新批评派的理论:比喻的本质不在比喻的两造,而在比喻关系中,如将 A 喻 B,A 与 B 的冲突可产生一个新的思想 X。

[2] 这里选译的是原诗第二章第四节。

On the real. This is the origin of change.
Winter and spring, cold copulars, embrace
And forth the particulars of rapture come.

Music falls on the silence like a sense,
A passion that we feel, not understand.
Morning and afternoon are clasped together

And North and South are an intrinsic couple
And sun and rain a plural, like two lovers
That walk away as one in the greenest body.

In solitude the trumpets of solitude
Are not of another solitude resounding;
A little string speaks for a crowd of voices.

The partaker partakes of that which changes him.
The child that touches takes character from the thing,
The body, it touches. The captain and his men

Are one and the sailor and the sea are one.
Follow after, O my companion, my fellow, my self,
Sister and solace, brother and delight.

1947

靠真实。这就是变化的根源。
冬与春,冰冷的联系,却在拥抱,
而欢乐的细节就从中出现。

音乐好像感觉落到寂静上,
这种激情我们能感受,却不理解。
早晨和下午相拥得那么紧,

北方和南方本是内在的一对,
阳光和雨复合,就像一对情人
漫步走去,变成一个最绿的身体。

这些孤独的号角在孤独中
并不是在回应另一种孤独;
一根细弦为一大群声音说话。

参与者参与使他们变化的事。
孩子触摸一个身体,一件东西,
就取得那种特征。船长和水手

是一个人,水手和大海是一体。
跟着我,哦,我的伙伴,我的朋友,我自身
是姐妹兼安慰,是兄弟兼欢乐。

1947

罗宾森·杰弗斯
(Robinson Jeffers, 1887-1962)

杰弗斯是现代美国诗坛一个思想和诗风都极为独特的诗人。他远离尘嚣,隐居在20世纪二三十年代还很荒凉的加利福尼亚太平洋海滨,在悬崖上的花岗岩房子中写出他那热情赞美大自然但却诅咒人类的独特诗篇。

杰弗斯早年游学欧洲,后到南加州大学攻读医学与文学。早在1912年他就出版过诗集,但因循陈词旧调,没有新意。1914年他开始避居于卡梅尔海滨,潜心摸索自己的诗路,十年后才出版诗集《塔马尔》,以其独特的风格轰动美国诗坛。此后他几乎每年都要出一本长诗与短诗的合集。1938年他那厚达700多页的《自选集》出版,达到他诗名的高峰。

他的诗中,大自然万象森列,奇景嵯峨,气势苍沛,充满力与运动。他的语言简朴明朗,诗风开阔。他对长句自由诗的节奏起伏掌握得尤其好。

但是这些描写大自然壮丽景色的诗,所要表达的却是杰弗斯自称为"非人道主义"的悲观主义。他赞美大自然是为了证明现代文明之堕落与生命短暂,这是一种尼采式的反进步的态度,一种否定社会的虚无主义。用杰弗斯自己的话来说,就是只有"摆脱人性,排除社会,融化于自然,人才能找到自己的价值,找到生命存在下去的意义甚至可能性"。

带着这样对人类绝望的悲观主义,他的创作走上窄路。20世纪40年代后他的诗作渐少,诗名式微,20世纪50年代他孤寂地度过余年。

然而,就杰弗斯所描写的大自然壮美景色的笔力而言,现代美国诗人很少有人能望其项背。

Divinely Superfluous Beauty

The storm-dances of gulls, the barking game of seals,
Over and under the ocean...
Divinely superfluous beauty
Rules the games, presides over destinies, makes trees
    grow
And hills tower, waves fall.
The incredible beauty of joy
Stars with fire the joining of lips, O let our loves too
Be joined, there is not a maiden
Burns and thirsts for love
More than my blood for you, by the shore of seals
    while the wings
Weave like a web in the air
Divinely superfluous beauty.

                                        1924

To the Stone-cutters

Stone-cutters fighting time with marble, you
    foredefeated

神圣的多余的美[1]

海鸥的暴风舞蹈,海豹的号叫比赛,

在海面上,在海水里……

神圣的多余的美,

控制比赛,君临命运,催树生长,

拔山巍耸,推浪倒倾。

欢乐,这难以置信的美

像燃烧的星,照耀着嘴唇的结合,哦让我们

  的爱也结合,没有一个

为爱而燃烧,为爱而饥渴的少女

比我的血对你的爱还要强烈的爱情,在海豹

  的岸边,正当翅膀

在空中像编网一样织出

神圣的多余的美。

1924

致凿石工

用大理石与时间斗争的凿石工,你们,命定

  要失败的

---

[1] "多余的美"是西方现代美学命题,认为艺术的真谛存在于对逻辑构架来说不必要的"多余的美"之中。

Challengers of oblivion

Eat cynical earnings, knowing rock splits, records
   fall down,

The square-limbed Roman letters

Scale in the thaws, wear in the rain. The poet as well

Builds his monument mockingly;

For man will be blotted out, the blithe earth die, the
   brave sun

Die blind and blacken to the heart:

Yet stones have stood for a thousand years, and
   pained thoughts found

The honey of peace in old poems.

                                                    1924

Summer Holiday

When the sun shouts and people abound

One thinks there were the ages of stone and the age
   of bronze

And the iron age; iron the unstable metal;

Steel made of iron, unstable as his mother; the
   towered-up cities

Will be stains of rust on mounds of plaster.

向忘却挑战的人,
你们勉强糊口,你们知道石头会碎裂,文字
　　记载会消失,
那方臂方腿的罗马字母
在解冻时剥落,在风雨中销蚀。诗人也同样
嘲弄似的建起他的纪念碑;
因为人类将被一笔勾销,欢乐的大地将死亡,
　　壮丽的太阳
将瞎了眼死去,透心发黑:
然而石碑已屹立千年,痛苦的思想
在古老的诗歌中找到安宁的蜜。

1924

夏天的假日

太阳狂呼,人头拥簇,
叫人想起曾经有石器时代,青铜时代,
也有铁器时代;铁,这不稳定的金属,
铁制的钢,不稳定一如其母;巍然高耸的
　　城市
将成为石灰堆上几点锈斑。

Roots will not pierce the heaps for a time, kind rains
    will cure them,
Then nothing will remain of the iron age
And all these people but a thigh-bone or so, a poem
Stuck in the world's thought, splinters of glass
In the rubbish dumps, a concrete dam far off in the
    mountain…

                                               1925

Gale in April

Intense and terrible beauty, how has our race with
    the frail naked nerves,
So little a craft swum down from its far launching?
Why now, only because the northwest blows and the
    headed grass billows,
Great seas jagging the west and on the granite
Blanching, the vessel is brimmed, this dancing play
    of the world is too much passion.
A gale in April so overfilling the spirit,
Though his ribs were thick as the earth's, arches of
    mountain, how shall one dare to live?

草根一时插不进，慈悲的雨能解决问题，
此后，铁器时代无物存留，
所有这些人，只剩一根大腿骨，一首诗
插在世界的思想上，像碎玻璃
混在垃圾堆里，混凝土坝远在深山之中……

1925

四月劲风

紧张而恐怖的美，我们这种族，神经脆弱裸露，
动作笨拙，怎么会从遥远的出发地游到此处？
就因为西北风猛吹，就因为长草垂头如波涛起伏，
大海刺戳着西岸，把花岗岩
洗得雪白，杯子满溢出来，世界的舞蹈游戏变得过
　　分热烈。
四月的一场劲风把精神装得太满，
哪怕他的肋骨像地球的山脉肋骨一样厚实，他敢活
　　下去？

Though his blood were like the earth's rivers and his
    flesh iron,
How shall one dare to live? One is born strong, how
    do the weak endure it?
The strong lean upon death as on a rock,
After eighty years there is shelter and the naked
    nerves shall be covered with deep quietness,
O beauty of things go on, go on, O torture
Of intense joy I have lasted out my time. I have
    thanked God and finished,
Roots of millennial trees fold me in the darkness,
Northwest wind shake their tops, not to the root,
    not to the root, I have passed
From beauty to the other beauty, peace, the night
    splendor.

1925

Hurt Hawks

I

The broken pillar of the wing jags from the clotted
    shoulder,
The wing trails like a banner in defeat,

哪怕他的血像大地的巨川,他的肉是铁,

他敢活下去?他生来是强者,弱者何能忍受?

强者倚在死亡上,就像靠住石头,

八十年后,就会得到掩蔽,裸露的神经就会盖上深厚的安宁。

哦,万物的美,继续下去,继续下去,哦,紧张的欢乐

那种折磨,我已经超越了我的生命,我感谢上帝,结束了一切。

千年巨树的根在黑暗中包裹着我。

西北风,摇撼树梢吧,但别摇根,别摇根,我已经从一种美

进入了另一种美,一种安宁,一种夜的壮丽。

1925

受伤的鹰

一

翅膀骨头从凝着血块的肩上撕开了,

拖曳着,像失败的旗帜,

No more to use the sky forever but live with famine
And pain a few days: cat nor coyote
Will shorten the week of waiting for death, there is
    game without talons.

He stands under the oak-bush and waits
The lame feet of salvation; at night he remembers
    freedom
And flies in a dream, the dawns ruin it.

He is strong and pain is worse to the strong,
    incapacity is worse.
The curs of the day come and torment him
At distance, no one but death the redeemer will
    humble that head,

The intrepid readiness, the terrible eyes.
The wild God of the world is sometimes merciful to
    those
That ask mercy, not often to the arrogant.

You do not know him, you communal people, or
    you have forgotten him;
Intemperate and savage, the hawk remembers him;

他再也用不着天空,只剩下几天的饥饿

和疼痛:没有猫,没有狼

来缩短这等死的一周,它们情愿找没爪的可口物。

他站在橡树丛下,等待着

拯救姗姗来迟;夜里,他想起昔日的自由,

他在梦中翱翔,但黎明打碎了梦。

他是强者,痛苦对强者来说更难熬,最难受的是

  无能为力。

白天野狗跑来,站在远处

折磨他,但只有死神这救星才能压弯这头颅,

这无畏的胆气、这恐怖的眼睛。

死,这位暴虐的人世之神对那些

乞怜者颇怀恻隐,对倨傲者常不容情。

群居的人们,你们不认识他,要不然就是忘了他;

但是桀骜不驯的鹰却记得他;

Beautiful and wild, the hawks, and men that are
 dying, remember him.

II

I'd sooner, except the penalties, kill a man than a
 hawk;
But the great redtail
Had nothing left but unable misery
From the bone too shattered for mending, the wing
 that trailed under his talons when he moved.

We had fed him six weeks, I gave him freedom,
He wandered over the foreland hill and returned in
 the evening, asking for death,
Not like a beggar, still eyed with the old
Implacable arrogance.

I gave him the lead gift in the twilight.
What fell was relaxed, Owl-downy, soft feminine
 feathers; but what
Soared: the fierce rush: the night-herons by the
 flooded river cried fear at its rising
Before it was quite unsheathed from reality.

1928

这些狂野而美丽的鹰,还有临死的人,都记得他。

二

要我杀一头鹰,我情愿杀人,只要不是行刑;
但这头巨大的红尾鹰
除了怅然的哀愁已一无所有,
骨头破裂已无法复原,走动时翅膀拖在脚后。

我们喂了他六周,最后我让他自由,
他在海岬的巉岩中徘徊了一天,晚上回来,请求一死,
但不是乞求,眼神中依然是
不可摧折的傲气。

在暮色中,我给了他铅制的礼物。
跌倒的是松弛的茸茸羽毛;但是
昂然升起的,是鹰的猛然冲刺:当它飞起,夜鹭在
　　涨水的河边恐惧地哇叫,
直到它从现实中脱颖而出,像利剑出鞘。

1928

Hands

Inside a cave in a narrow canyon near Tassajara
The vault of rock is painted with hands,
A multitude of hands in the twilight, a cloud of men's
    palms, no more,
No other picture. There's no one to say
Whether the brown shy quiet people who are dead
    intended
Religion or magic, or made their tracings
In the idleness of art; but over the division of years
    these careful
Signs-manual are now like a sealed message
Saying: "Look: we also were human; we had hands,
    not paws. All hail
You people with the cleverer hands, our supplanters
In the beautiful country; enjoy her a season, her
    beauty, and come down
And be supplanted; for you also are human."

1929

手

塔沙加拉附近狭窄的峡谷中有个洞穴,
岩石的圆穹上画满了手,
幽暗的光照出无数的手,手掌的云,其余
   什么也没画。没人能说出
那些已消逝的羞怯的棕色种族想表现的
是宗教?是巫术?还是仅仅在空闲时
从事艺术,留下这些痕迹?但是无数世代之后,
这些仔细画下的手势符号已变成密封的信息。
它们在说:"瞧:我们也是人;我们有手,不是爪子。
   欢迎你们
手指更为灵巧的人,在这个美丽的国土上
接替我们的人;享受她的美吧,享受一个季节,
   然后倒下吧,
让别的人接替你们;因为你们也是人。"

                                    1929

Evening Ebb

The ocean has not been so quiet for a long while;
    five night-herons
Fly shorelong voiceless in the hush of the air
Over the calm of an ebb that almost mirrors their
    wings.
The sun has gone down, and the water has gone down
From the weed-clad rock, but the distant cloud-wall
    rises. The ebb whispers.
Great cloud-shadows float in the opal water.
Through rifts in the screen of the world pale gold
    gleams, and the evening
Star suddenly glides like a flying torch.
As if we had not been meant to see her; rehearsing
    behind
The screen of the world for another audience.

                                                  1929

晚间退潮

大海很久没这样宁静;五只夜鹭
在沉寂的空中沿海岸悄然飞去,
掠过,几乎映出倒影的平静水面。
太阳和海水,都从长满水草的岩礁上
落了下去,但远方的云墙升起。退潮的大海低语。
巨大的云影在猫眼石般的水面上漂浮。
而从世界之幕的缝隙中,淡金色的光辉带着
夜晚的星群,突然泻出,有如飞翔的火炬,
看来并非有心在我们眼前露面,他们原是在世界
这幕的后面,为另一批观众排演。

1929

New Mexican Mountain

I watch the Indians dancing to help the young corn
    at Taos pueblo. The old men squat in a ring
And make the song, the young women with fat bare
    arms, and a few shame-faced young men, shuffle
    the dance.

The lean-muscled young men are naked to the
    narrow loins, their breasts and backs daubed with
    white clay,
Two eagle-feathers plume the black heads. They
    dance with reluctance, they are growing civilized;
    the old men persuade them.

Only the drum is confident, it thinks the world has
    not changed; the beating heart, the simplest of
    rhythms,
It thinks the world has not changed at all; it is only a
    dreamer, a brainless heart, the drum has no eyes.

These tourists have eyes, the hundred watching
    the dance, white Americans, hungrily too, with
    reverence, not laughter;

新墨西哥山中

我在陶斯[1]人那里看印第安人跳催禾舞。老人们蹲着,围一个圈
唱着歌,年轻女人裸着肥硕的胳臂,一些腼颜的年轻人穿梭舞蹈。

肌肉精瘦的年轻人赤裸到腿弯,胸前背后涂着白泥,
黑头发上插两支鹰羽,他们不太情愿地跳着,他们渐渐文明化,但老人们硬要他们跳。

只有鼓是自信的,它认为世界毫无变化;那搏动的心脏,那最简朴的节奏,
它认为世界毫无变化;它是一个梦想家,一个无头脑的心脏,鼓没有眼睛。

但旅游者有眼睛,上百人围看舞蹈,白皮肤的美国人,贪婪地看着,满怀崇敬,没人想笑;

---

[1] 新墨西哥州一山区,此处有印第安人"保留区"。

Pilgrims from civilization, anxiously seeking beauty,
religion, poetry; pilgrims from the vacuum.

People from cities, anxious to be human again. Poor
show how they suck you empty! The Indians are
emptied,
And certainly there was never religion enough, nor
beauty nor poetry here... to fill Americans.

Only the drum is confident, it thinks the world
has not changed. Apparently only myself and the
strong
Tribal drum, and the rockhead of Taos mountain,
remember that civilization is a transient sickness.

1933

Love the Wild Swan

"I hate my verses, every line, every word.
Oh pale and brittle pencils ever to try
One grass-blade's curve, or the throat of one bird
That clings to twig, ruffled against white sky.
Oh cracked and twilight mirrors ever to catch

朝拜者来自文明之邦，渴求美、宗教、诗歌；朝拜者来自真空。

城市里来的人，渴望重新取得人性。好个丑相，他们把你们吸干！印第安人被吸干，
当然那里没有足够的宗教、美或诗歌……来填饱美国人。

只有鼓是自信的，它认为世界没有变化。看来只有我自己和这部落的
有力的鼓，以及陶斯山的岩石巨面还记得，文明是一种旋生旋灭的疾病。

1933

爱野天鹅

"我恨自己的诗，每一行，每一个字，
哦，铅笔多么苍白脆弱，它想试试
一条草叶的曲线，一只攀着树枝
或掠过空阔长天的飞鸟的嗓子。
哦，模糊的破镜，它想要抓住

One color, one glinting

Hash, of the splendor of things.

Unlucky hunter, Oh bullets of wax,

The lion beauty, the wild-swan wings, the storm of the wings."

—This wild swan of a world is no hunter's game.

Better bullets than yours would miss the white breast

Better mirrors than yours would crack in the flame.

Does it matter whether you hate your... self?

At least Love your eyes that can see, your mind that can

Hear the music, the thunder of the wings. Love the wild swan.

1935

Shine, Perishing Republic

While this America settles in the mould of its vulgarity, heavily thickening to empire

And protest, only a bubble in the molten mass, pops and sighs out, and the mass hardens,

壮美世界的,

一种颜色,一条光影,

没交好运的猎人,哦,蜡做的子弹,

狮子的美,野天鹅的翼,翅翼的暴风。"

——这野天鹅属于世界,不会让人猎获,

比你好的子弹打不中那白胸脯,

比你好的镜子在火中也会开裂,

你恨你……自己?都没所谓。至少

爱你能看见的眼,能听翅膀击搏

这雷鸣似的音乐的心。爱野天鹅。

1935

闪耀吧,正在朽败的共和国

看到这个美国在庸俗的模子里成型,厚厚地凝结成帝国,

抗议只是溶液中的一个水泡,破裂了,叹口气,而大团物质变硬,

I sadly smiling remember that the flower fades to
    make fruit, the fruit rots to make earth.
Out of the mother; and through the spring exultances,
    ripeness and decadence; and home to the mother.

You making haste haste on decay: not blameworthy;
    life is good, be it stubbornly long or suddenly
A mortal splendor: meteors are not needed less than
    mountains: shine, perishing republic.

But for my children, I would have them keep their
    distance from the thickening center; corruption
Never has been compulsory, when the cities lie at
    the monster's feet there are left the mountains.

And boys, be in nothing so moderate as in love of
    man, a clever servant, insufferable master.
There is the trap that catches noblest spirits, that
    caught—they say—God, when he walked on
    earth.

                                              1935

这时我悲伤地微笑，我想到花凋萎成果实，果实
　　腐烂成泥土。
来自母亲；经过春日的欢乐、成熟和朽败；又回
　　向母亲。

你急急忙忙地腐烂：做得不错；生活是美好的，
　　不管它长得死皮赖脸，还是像
瞬息而逝的闪光：需要山，也需要流星：闪耀吧，
　　正在朽败的共和国。

至于我的孩子，我让他们远离那越来越黏厚的中
　　心；腐朽
决不会强加于人；当城市匍匐在妖魔脚下，山依
　　然屹立。

孩子们，不要做爱别人那样低声下气的事，聪明
　　的奴仆正是最骄横的主人。
有一个陷阱专门抓捕最崇高的灵魂，据说，当上
　　帝走上地球，就已经被抓住。

1935

Clouds of Evening

Enormous cloud-mountains that form over Point
    Lobos and into the sunset,
Figures of fire on the walls of to-night's storm,
Foam of gold in gorges of fire, and the great file of
    warrior angels:
Dreams gathering in the curded brain of the earth,
The sky the brain-vault, on the threshold of sleep:
    poor earth, you like your children
By inordinate desires tortured make dreams?
Storms more enormous, wars nobler, more toppling
    mountains, more jewelled waters, more free
Fires on impossible headlands... as a poor girl
Wishing her lover taller and more desirous, and
    herself maned with gold,
Dreams the world right, in the cold bed, about dawn.
Dreams are beautiful; the slaves of form are beautiful
    also; I have grown to believe
A stone is a better pillow than many visions.

                                         1935

晚云

宏伟的云山在洛沃斯角上空堆积,化成晚霞,
　　在今夜风暴的墙上绘出燃烧的图画,
火的峡谷中金色的浪花,大队的天国武士:
　　梦在大地凝冻的脑子中聚集——
天空是这脑子的颅壳——在睡眠的门槛上:
　　可怜的大地,你难道和你的孩子一样
也被无法克制的欲望折磨着,也得做梦?
奢望更宏大的风暴,更壮观的战场,更陡峭的山
　　峰,更晶莹的水流,更自由的
火焰,在这不可能的海岬上……就像一个可怜的
　　姑娘
希望她的爱人更高大,更英俊,而她自己有金色
　　的秀发,
她梦到一切如意,在冰冷的床上,当天甫黎明。
梦是美的;形式的奴隶也是美的。我开始相信
一块石头是比许多美景更好的枕头。

　　　　　　　　　　　　　　1935

Grey Weather

It is true that, older than man and ages to outlast
   him, the Pacific surf
Still cheerfully pounds the worn granite drum;
But there's no storm; and the birds are still, no song;
   no kind of excess;
Nothing that shines, nothing is dark;
There; is neither joy nor grief nor a person, the sun's
   tooth sheathed in cloud,
And life has no more desires than a stone.
The stormy conditions of time and change are all
   abrogated, the essential
Violences of survival, pleasure,
Love, wrath and pain, and the curious desire of
   knowing, all perfectly suspended.
In the cloudy light, in the timeless quietness,
One explores deeper than the nerves or heart of
   nature, the womb or soul,
To the bone, the careless white bone, the excellence.

                                                    1935

灰蒙蒙的天气

确实,比人,比岁月长寿得多,这太平洋的巨涛
仍在兴高采烈地捶击已磨蚀的花岗岩鼓;
但这里没有暴雨;鸟静静地飞,没有歌声;没有任何放纵;
没有光亮之处,也没有幽暗之物;
这里,没有欢乐,没有悲伤,也没有人,太阳的牙齿镶裹在云里,
而生命不比一块石头有更多的欲望。
沧桑变化那暴风雨般的力量被剥夺,那对生存
至关重要的暴力,那欢乐,
爱情,愤怒,痛苦以及好奇的求知欲,一切都彻底中止。
在云层透出的光里,在无时间的静谧中,
人能探寻到比神经,比人性的心脏,比子宫和灵魂更深沉处,
直探到骨头,无忧无虑的白骨,那精美绝伦之处。

1935

Rock and Hawk

Here is a symbol in which
Many high tragic thoughts
Watch their own eyes.

This gray rock, standing tall
On the headland, where the sea-wind
Lets no tree grow,

Earthquake-proved, and signatured
By ages of storms: on its peak
A falcon has perched.

I think, here is your emblem
To hang in the future sky;
Not the cross, not the hive,

But this; bright power, dark peace;
Fierce consciousness joined with final
Disinterestedness;

Life with calm death; the falcon's
Realist eyes and act
Married to the massive

岩和鹰

这是一个象征,在这里
许多崇高而悲壮的思想
凝视着自己的眼睛。

这灰色巨岩,巍然屹立
在海角尖上,在这里,海风
不让任何树生长。

地震无奈它何,无数世纪的
暴风雨签下了名:在它顶上
一只鹰隼栖落。

我想这就是你的标志
可悬挂在未来的天空;
不用十字架或蜂窝,

就用这;光辉的力,幽暗的静;
激昂的意识与最终的
冷漠携手并进;

生命和安详的死;鹰的
现实主义的眼光和动作
结合了岩石

Mysticism of stone,

Which failure cannot cast down

Nor success make proud.

1935

Watch the Lights Fade

Gray steel, cloud-shadow-stained,
The ocean takes the last lights of evening.
Loud is the voice and the foam lead-color,
And flood-tide devours the sands.

Here stand, like an old stone,
And watch the lights fade and hear the sea's voice.
Hate and despair take Europe and Asia,
And the sea-wind blows cold.

Night comes: night will claim all.
The world is not changed, only more naked:
The strong struggle for power, and the weak
Warm their poor hearts with hate.

那魁伟厚实的神秘主义,

失败无法使它丧气

成功也不会使它骄傲。

1935

暮望[1]

灰色的钢,沾满阴云的色彩,

大海取走晚上最后的光线。

震耳的声音,铅灰的浪花,

海潮吞没了沙滩。

我站着,像块老石头,

凝视着天光消失,听着海声。

仇恨和失望抓住欧洲和亚洲,

而海风吹来寒气。

夜来了:夜要求一切。

世界没变,只是更加赤裸:

强者为权力格斗,而弱者

用仇恨温暖心房。

---

[1] 杰弗斯对第二次世界大战持孤立主义态度,反对美国参战,这首诗暴露出他的立场。

Night comes: come into the house,

Try around the dial for a late news-cast.

These others are America's voices: naive and

Powerful; spurious; doom-touched.

How soon? Four years or forty?

Why should an old stone pick at the future?

Stand on your shore, old stone, be still while the

Sea-wind salts your head white.

1941

夜来了:走进屋内,

转着旋钮,想听最新消息。

这些就是美国之声:天真烂漫,

有力;骗人;沾上死亡。

多久? 四年? 四十年?

为何一块老石头要挑拣未来?

站在岸上,老石头,静静地,让那

海风的盐吹白你的头。

1941

E. E. 肯明斯
(Edward Estlin Cummings, 1894-1962)

肯明斯是现代美国诗坛一个引人注目的人物,这首先是由于他在诗歌形式上的大胆实验:字母一般用小写,有时在奇怪的地方冒出个大写字母,几乎取消标点,任意折句甚至拆字,不顾语法、句法而搞文字游戏,因此他似乎是一个非常"现代派"的诗人。但实际上他只是一个文字形式上的现代派,他乐此不疲的题材是爱情和春天,他玩世不恭的诗的核心是追求个性的自由,因此他的诗在内容上是浪漫主义传统的继承。他的诗要表达的意思并不隐晦,主题有时并不深刻,但他在实验形式的同时保持了一种抒情气质。

肯明斯很早就开始写诗。1917年,他志愿参加救护队去欧陆战场,却被法国当局当成奸细关押起来。他以这段经历为题材写成长篇小说《大房间》,此书成为战后"迷惘的一代"的首批作品之一。

20世纪20年代初他的独特诗风形成,自1923年出版《郁金香与烟囱》后,他先后发表了十多本诗集,一直沿用这种诗风。这种古怪诗体在20世纪二三十年代,甚至在今天,都颇受讥议,但同时也得到许多人的喜爱,而且还吸引了不少国家的模仿者。

肯明斯还是个画家,在巴黎和纽约都举行过个人画展。他的画风接近立体主义,这对他的特殊诗风的形成也有一定影响。

肯明斯的某些诗在字形上过于追求花样,无法翻译,但这类诗并不多。本诗集所收译诗,努力用汉语模仿肯明斯拆散英文词形或句法的效果,成败与否,读者鉴之。

in Just—

in Just—
spring   when the world is mud-
luscious the little
lame balloonman

whistles   far   and   wee

and eddieandbill come
running from marbles and
piracies and it's
spring

when the world is puddle-wonderful

the queer
old balloonman whistles
far   and   wee
and bettyandisbel come dancing

from hop-scotch and jump-rope and

it's
spring
and

正是——

正是——
大好春光　　世界充满烂泥
的芳香那小个儿
跛脚的卖气球人

吹着口哨　远远地　嘘嘘地

埃迪比尔俩来了
抛开了弹子和
抓强盗游戏奔过来这是
大好春光

当世界处处水潭多带劲

那古怪的
卖气球老头吹着口哨
远远地　嘘嘘地
贝蒂伊斯倍俩一路舞过来

抛开造房子和跳绳游戏

这是
春天
而

                the

                        goat-footed

        balloonMan   whistles
        far
        and
        wee
                                        1923

Spring is like a perhaps hand

      Spring is like a perhaps hand
      (which comes carefully
      out of Nowhere)arranging
      a window, into which people look(while
      people stare
      arranging and changing placing
      carefully there a strange
      thing and a known thing here)and

      changing everything carefully

　　　　那个

　　　　　　山羊脚的 [1]

　　　卖气球人　吹着口哨
　　　远远地
　　　且
　　　嘘嘘地

　　　　　　　　　　　　1923

春天像一只或许的手

春天像一只或许的手
(小心地来自
乌有) 布置
一面橱窗, 给人张望 (让
人们看着它
小心翼翼地布置
调换位置, 这里一件
陌生的那里一件熟悉的) 而且

小心地变换每件东西

1　希腊神话中的牧神是人身羊腿。

spring is like a perhaps
Hand in a window
(carefully to
and fro moving New and
Old things,while
people stare carefully
moving a perhaps
fraction of flower here placing
an inch of air there)and

without breaking anything.

1925

Humanity i love you

Humanity i love you
because you would rather black the boots of
success than enquire whose soul dangles from his
watch-chain which would be embarrassing for both

parties and because you
unflinchingly applaud all

春天像一只或许的

手在橱窗里

（小心地来来

回回搬动新的和

旧的东西，让人们

仔细看着它

移来一个或许的

花的碎片，搬走

一时空气）而且

决不会打破任何东西。

1925

人类我爱你

人类我爱你

因为你情愿给成功擦皮靴

不问他的表带上晃荡的

是谁的灵魂那会使双方

难堪而且因为你

在老霍华德[1]听到每支

---
1 纽约一剧场名。

songs containing the words country home and
mother when sung at the old howard

Humanity i love you because
when you're hard up you pawn your
intelligence to buy a drink and when
you're flush pride keeps

you from the pawn shop and
because you are continually committing
nuisances but more
especially in your own house

Humanity i love you because you
are perpetually putting the secret of
life in your pants and forgetting
it's there and sitting down

on it
and because you are
forever making poems in the lap
of death Humanity

i hate you

                                                             1925

歌曲都坚定地鼓掌只要
里头有祖国母亲这类词儿

人类我爱你因为你
日子不好过时把理智
押进当铺买酒喝而
脸色绯红时自尊心又

让你不敢靠近当铺而且
因为你老是不断地闹出
乱子但大部分
还是在你自己家里

人类我爱你因为你
不断地把生命的秘密
放进裤衩又老是忘记
一屁股坐

到上面
而且因为你
永远在死的股掌之中
吟诗作赋人类

我恨你

1925

since feeling is first

since feeling is first
who pays any attention
to the syntax of things
will never wholly kiss you;

wholly to be a fool
while Spring is in the world

my blood approves,
and kisses are a better fate
than wisdom
lady i swear by all flowers.   Don't cry
—the best gesture of my brain is less than
your eyelids' flutter which says

we are for each other: then
laugh, leaning back in my arms
for life's not a paragraph

And death i think is no parenthesis

1926

既然感情第一

既然感情第一
那么留意于
事物句法的人
就不会好好吻你;

当世上春光明媚
我的血赞成

好好做个傻瓜,
而吻是比智慧
更好的命运
姑娘我以所有的花的名义起誓。　别哭
——我头脑中最妙的姿势
比不上你眼睑一眨,因为它说明

我们互相倾心:那么
大笑,在我臂弯中仰身
因为生活不是一个段落

因为死亡我认为不是括弧

1926

next to of course god america i

"next to of course god america i
love you land of the pilgrims' and so forth oh
say can you see by the dawn's early my
country 'tis of centuries come and go
and are no more what of it we should worry
in every language even deafanddumb
thy sons acclaim your glorious name by gorry
by jingo by gee by gosh by gum
why talk of beauty what could be more beautiful than these heroic happy dead
who rushed like lions to the roaring slaughter
they did not stop to think they died instead
then shall the voice of liberty be mute?"
He spoke.   And drank rapidly a glass of water

1926

当然仅仅次于上帝美国我

"当然仅仅次于上帝美国我

爱你这朝圣者的土地[1]云云哦

例如你能在晨光中见到我的

国家几个世纪的忙忙碌碌

再没别的我们有何可担心

用各种语言哪怕聋子哑巴

你的儿子欢呼你名字喊着

哎呀噢嗬啊咦嗳嗨呜呼

还谈什么美有什么能比这些

英勇的快乐的死者更加壮美

他们像狮子冲进呼啸的屠场

没停下想一想就一死了之

所以自由的声音难道会消失?"

他说着。 猛喝下一大杯水

1926

---

[1] 美国早期移民多为逃避宗教迫害而从英国迁来的清教徒,他们自称"朝圣者"。

my sweet old etcetera

my sweet old etcetera
aunt lucy during the recent

war could and what
is more did tell you just
what everybody was fighting

for,
my sister

isabel created hundreds
(and
hundreds)of socks not to
mention shirts fleaproof earwarmers

etcetera wristers etcetera, my
mother hoped that

i would die etcetera
bravely of course my father used
to become hoarse talking about how it was
a privilege and if only he
could meanwhile my

我那可爱的如此等等

我那可爱的如此等等
老婶妈露西在最近几年

战争期间能够而且
主要的确告诉人们
每个人都在为何

而战,
我的妹妹

伊莎贝尔做了几百只
(外加
几百只)袜子还别提
衬衫防虱子的耳套

如此等等护腕如此等等,我的
母亲希望

我死得如此等等
勇敢当然我的父亲一向是
谈得唇焦舌敝那是
一种特权只要他
还能上阵,而此时我

self etcetera lay quietly

in the deep mud et

cetera

(dreaming,

et

cetera, of

Your smile

eyes knees and of your Etcetera)

1926

somewhere i have never travelled, gladly beyond

somewhere i have never travelled,gladly beyond
any experience,your eyes have their silence:
in your most frail gesture are things which enclose me,
or which i cannot touch because they are too near

your slightest look easily will unclose me
though i have closed myself as fingers,
you open always petal by petal myself as Spring opens
(touching skilfully,mysteriously)her first rose

自己如此等等静静躺在

深深的泥浆里如此

等等

(梦想着

如此

等等,想着

你的微笑

眼睛膝盖和你的如此等等)

1926

有个地方我从未去过,在经验之外

有个地方我从未去过,在经验之外

愉快地存在,你的眼睛有种沉默:

你最纤巧的姿态里有东西能紧裹我,

也有东西太靠近我使我无法触摸

哪怕我把自己关紧像捏拢手指

你最轻微的目光也很容易打开我,

一瓣儿一瓣儿开,就像春天打开

(巧妙、神秘地触摸着)第一朵玫瑰

or if your wish be to close me,i and
my life will shut very beautifully,suddenly,
as when the heart of this flower imagines
the snow carefully everywhere descending;

nothing which we are to perceive in this world equals
the power of your intense fragility:whose texture
compels me with the colour of its countries,
rendering death and forever with each breathing

(i do not know what it is about you that closes
and opens;only something in me understands
the voice of your eyes is deeper than all roses)
nobody,not even the rain,has such small hands

1931

anyone lived in a pretty how town

anyone lived in a pretty how town
(with up so floating many bells down)
spring summer autumn winter
he sang his didn't he danced his did.

或者你的愿望是把我关起,我和
我的生命会关闭,优美地,突然地,
似乎这朵花的心里正在想象
漫天白雪小心翼翼处处飘下;

这世界上我们理解的东西没一件
能与你紧绷的纤巧相比:那种质地
用它本乡的颜色逼迫着我,
给我死亡而且永远地随着每次呼吸

(我不知道你有什么本领能开
又能关;我心中却有东西能够
理解你眼睛的声音深于任何玫瑰)
没人,哪怕雨,也没有如此小巧的手

1931

任何人住在一个多美小城

任何人住在一个多美小城
(往上飘的声往下摇的钟)
春花夏叶秋月冬雪
他唱不做的事,他跳他做的事。

Women and men(both little and small)
cared for anyone not at all
they sowed their isn't they reaped their same
sun moon stars rain

children guessed(but only a few
and down they forgot as up they grew
autumn winter spring summer)
that noone loved him more by more

when by now and tree by leaf
she laughed his joy she cried his grief
bird by snow and stir by still
anyone's any was all to her

someones married their everyones
laughed their cryings and did their dance
(sleep wake hope and then)they
said their nevers they slept their dream

stars rain sun moon
(and only the snow can begin to explain
how children are apt to forget to remember
with up so floating many bells down)

女人和男人（都是小不点点）
根本不把任何人放在心间
他们播种不是，收的却一回事
太阳月亮星辰雨点

孩子都来猜题（只有几个猜着
一面往上长大，一面朝下忘记
秋月冬雪春花夏叶）
没有人越来越喜欢他这个人

何时靠如今，大树靠绿叶
女为男喜而笑，女为男恼而泣
飞鸟靠飞雪，动弹靠安定
任何人的任何对她都是一切

有的人与每个人都可做夫妇
笑出他们的哭跳出他们的舞
（睡觉醒来希望然后）他们
说自己的永不，睡自己的梦境

星辰雨点太阳月亮
（只有白雪能开始说明
为何孩子容易忘记去记
随着声音往上飘钟儿往下摇）

one day anyone died i guess

(and noone stooped to kiss his face)

busy folk buried them side by side

little by little and was by was

all by all and deep by deep

and more by more they dream their sleep

noone and anyone earth by april

wish by spirit and if by yes.

Women and men(both dong and ding)

summer autumn winter spring

reaped their sowing and went their came

sun moon stars rain

                                        1940

love is more thicker than forget

love is more thicker than forget

more thinner than recall

more seldom than a wave is wet

more frequent than to fail

某天任何人死去我这么猜想
（没人会俯下身来吻他脸庞）
忙碌的人们把他们并排埋下
一点随着一点，过去跟着过去

所有加上所有，深沉加上深沉
更多加上更多，他们睡眠做梦
没人加任何人，大地加上四月
愿望加上精神，如果加上就是

女人和男人（都是咚和叮）
夏叶秋月冬雪春花
收获他们种的，走回他们来处
太阳月亮星辰雨点

1940

爱情比忘却厚

爱情比忘却厚
比回忆薄
比潮湿的波浪少
比失败多

it is most mad and moonly
and less it shall unbe
than all the sea which only
is deeper than the sea

love is less always than to win
less never than alive
less bigger than the least begin
less littler than forgive

it is most sane and sunly
and more it cannot die
than all the sky which only
is higher than the sky

1940

plato told

plato told

him:he couldn't
believe it(jesus

它最痴癫最疯狂

也比起所有

比海洋更深的海洋

它更为长久

爱情总比胜利少见

却比活着多些

不大于无法开始

不小于谅解

它最明朗最清醒

而比起所有

比天空更高的天空

它更为不朽

1940

柏拉图对他

柏拉图对他

说过：他没法

相信（耶稣

told him;he

wouldn't believe

it)lao

tsze

certainly told

him,and general

(yes

mam)

sherman;

and even

(believe it

or

not)you

told him:i told

him;we told him

(he didn't believe it,no

sir)it took

a nipponized bit of

the old sixth

对他说过；他

不愿相信

这事）老

子当然也对他

说过，还有

将军[1]

（没错

太太）

谢尔曼

甚至还有

（信

或

不信）你

也对他说过；我也

对他说过；我们都对他说过

（他根本不信，是啊

先生）非得

把一块日本化的

第六

---

[1] W. T. 谢尔曼（1820—1891），美国南北战争时北军著名将领。

avenue

el;in the top of his head:to tell

him

                              1944

let it go—the

      let it go—the
      smashed word broken
      open vow or
      the oath cracked length
      wise—let it go it
      was sworn to

              go

      let them go—the
      truthful liars and
      the false fair friends
      and the boths and
      neithers—you must let them go they

街

旧高架铁轨;[1] 放进他的脑袋:就这么告诉

他

1944

让它走——这

让它走——这
破碎的词背弃的
公开誓言或
裂开长口的保证
聪明些——让它走它
赌过咒要
　　　　　走

让他们走——这
忠实的撒谎者和
虚假的好朋友
这两人一个也
不要——你得让他们走他们

---

[1] 20世纪30年代后期美国将废铁(包括刚拆除的纽约第六街高架电车)卖给日本制造军火。

             were born

                          to go

             let all go—the

             big small middling

             tall bigger really

             the biggest and all

             things—let all go

             dear

                          so comes love

                                              1944

when life is quite through with

             when life is quite through with

             and leaves say alas,

             much is to do

             for the swallow,that closes

             a flight in the blue;

             when love's had his tears out,

             perhaps shall pass

             a million years

生来就是
　　　　要走

让全部人都走——这
大的小的中等的
真正高大更大的
最最大的和其他
一切——让全部人都走
亲爱的
　　　　爱情这才会来

　　　　　　　　　　1944

当生命已经告终

当生命已经告终
当树叶叹一声：唉，
对那在蓝天里
结束了飞行的燕子来说
还有不少事要做；

当爱情流干眼泪，
可能还要经过
一百万年

                (while a bee dozes

                on the poppies, the dears;

                when all's done and said,and

                under the grass

                lies her head

                by oaks and roses

                deliberated.)

                                              1944

when faces called flowers float out of the ground

   when faces called flowers float out of the ground
   and breathing is wishing and wishing is having—
   but keeping is downward and doubting and never
   —it's april(yes,april;my darling)it's spring!
   yes the pretty birds frolic as spry as can fly
   yes the little fish gambol as glad as can be
   (yes the mountains are dancing together)

   when every leaf opens without any sound
   and wishing is having and having is giving—
   but keeping is doting and nothing and nonsense
   —alive;we're alive,dear:it's(kiss me now)spring!

（正是一只蜜蜂

在可爱的罂粟花上，打瞌睡的时间；

正是一切做完，一切说完，而且

她的头

躺在草下

傍着橡树，依着玫瑰，

静思凝神。）

1944

当称作花朵的面容从大地浮起

当称作花朵的面容从大地浮起

而呼吸是希望而希望是拥有——

但保持却是下落是怀疑是永不

——这是四月（是呵，四月；亲爱的）是春天！

是呵美丽的鸟儿飞得多么轻捷

是呵小巧的鱼儿嬉戏兴高采烈

（是呵山岭都在一起舞蹈）

当每片叶子轻轻打开无声无息

而希望就是拥有而拥有就是给予——

但保持却是昏庸是乌有是胡扯

——快活；我们快活，亲爱的：这是（现在吻我）春天！

now the pretty birds hover so she and so he

now the little fish quiver so you and so i

(now the mountains are dancing, the mountains)

when more than was lost has been found has been found

and having is giving and giving is living—

but keeping is darkness and winter and cringing

—it's spring(all our night becomes day)o, it's spring!

all the pretty birds dive to the heart of the sky

all the little fish climb through the mind of the sea

(all the mountains are dancing;are dancing)

           1950

瞧呵美丽的鸟儿高翔像她和他

瞧呵小巧的鱼儿战栗像你和我

（瞧呵山岭在舞蹈，山岭）

当失去的少找到的多找到的多

而拥有就是给予而给予就是生活——

但保持却是黑暗是冬天是皱缩

——是春天（我们的夜都成了白昼）呵，是春天！

所有美丽的鸟儿潜入天空的心房

所有小巧的鱼儿爬进大海的灵魂

（所有的山岭都在狂舞；都在狂舞）

           1950

哈特·克兰
(Hart Crane, 1899-1932)

哈特·克兰，这位33岁投海自杀的诗歌奇才，至今在美国仍享有盛誉。

自童年起，不幸就跟着他：父母反目，长年争吵，离婚后母亲因精神病被送进医院。中学辍学后，他一面开始写诗，一面寻找各种职业谋生。后来他潦倒酗酒，放浪无度，四处为家，永无安定。生活造就了他孤僻奇特的性格，17岁时他就开始发表诗作，至20岁他已是一名有经验的诗人了。当艾略特的《荒原》出版后，克兰反对此诗中把现代生活描写成完全丧失希望的时代，他要写出"一个更加积极的现代社会"，于是他花七年时间写出毕生力作《桥》。"桥"指的是纽约的布鲁克林大桥，他力图用充满活力的纽约对比艾略特笔下沦为"荒原"的伦敦，想写出在他心中浮现的"美国神话"。1930年，长诗出版，反响不大。全诗虽结构松散，交织着朦胧的希望和失望感，但仍有一些非常美的片段。

克兰的诗广泛使用象征和暗示，形象奇美，色彩瑰丽，有时古怪奇谲，很难索解。他的诗和他匆匆自我了结的生活一样奇特。他在诗中努力把惠特曼的豪迈开阔和爱伦·坡的神秘主义结合起来，以表现现代城市的精神。从他留在世上的薄薄几本诗集推测，他本应有一个成果丰富的诗歌前程。克兰自杀后，尽管新批评派如退特等人曾大力推荐他的力作《桥》，但都没有大获成功，这或许也说明了：在现代，惠特曼式的对科学与民主的美国的希望注定破灭，当前的文明已无法容纳乐观主义的浩歌。

My Grandmother's Love Letters

There are no stars tonight
But those of memory.
Yet how much room for memory there is
In the loose girdle of soft rain.

There is even room enough
For the letters of my mother's mother,
Elizabeth,
That have been pressed so long
Into a corner of the roof
That they are brown and soft,
And liable to melt as snow.

Over the greatness of such space
Steps must be gentle.
It is all hung by an invisible white hair.
It trembles as birch limbs webbing the air.

And I ask myself:

"Are your fingers long enough to play
Old keys that are but echoes:

外婆的情书 [1]

今夜没有星星

只有回忆之星。

可是细雨缠绵下

多少事让人回忆。

甚至还让人想起

我母亲的母亲

伊丽莎白写的信,

在屋顶下的角落

塞了多少年

早已发黄变脆,

随时会化掉,像雪。

时间那么遥远

脚步必须放轻。

信悬于一根看不见的白发,

颤抖,像白桦树枝在风中织网。

我问自己:

"你的手指那么长

能弹已成回音的琴键吗:

---

1 这是克兰的一首代表诗作,于 1920 年刊于《日晷》杂志。

Is the silence strong enough

To carry back the music to its source

And back to you again

As though to her?"

Yet I would lead my grandmother by the hand

Through much of what she would not understand;

And so I stumble. And the rain continues on the roof

With such a sound of gently pitying laughter.

1926

Black Tambourine

The interests of a black man in a cellar

Mark tardy judgment on the world's closed door.

Gnats toss in the shadow of a bottle,

And a roach spans a crevice in the floor.

Æsop, driven to pondering, found

Heaven with the tortoise and the hare;

Fox brush and sow ear top his grave

And mingling incantations on the air.

寂静的力量那么强

能把音乐带回声源

再传回给你

就像传给她?"

但是我还得拉着外婆的手

领她穿过那么多她不懂的东西;

我迟疑。雨依旧打着屋顶

那声音像怜悯的笑,很轻。

1926

黑手鼓[1]

地窖中黑人的利益在世界

关着的门上看到迟延的判决。

蚊蚋在瓶子的阴影里折腾,

蟑螂测量着地板上的缝隙。

伊索,被迫思考,他发现了

一个有龟,有兔的天堂;

狐尾和猪耳长在他的坟头

把神秘的咒文混入风中。

---

[1] 克兰曾在他父亲所开饭馆的地下储藏室工作过一段时间,这饭馆有个黑人跑堂。克兰说他写这首诗是为表达黑人处于"人与兽之间的地位"。

The black man, forlorn in the cellar,

Wanders in some mid-kingdom, dark, that lies,

Between his tambourine, stuck on the wall,

And, in Africa, a carcass quick with flies.

1926

North Labrador

A land of leaning ice

Hugged by plaster-grey arches of sky,

Flings itself silently

Into eternity.

"Has no one come here to win you,

Or left you with the faintest blush

Upon your glittering breasts?

Have you no memories, O Darkly Bright?"

Cold-hushed, there is only the shifting moments

That journey toward no Spring—

No birth, no death, no time nor sun

In answer.

1926

那黑人,被抛弃在地窖里,

在一个黑暗的中央王国漫游,

一边是他挂在墙上的手鼓,

一边是在非洲很快长蛆的尸首。

1926

北拉布拉多[1]

巨冰倾斜的土地
被石膏般灰白的天空拥在怀里,
把自己静静地
抛入永恒。

"从来没人来赢取你,
或者让你闪光的
胸脯上微微起点红晕?
你没记忆吗,哦黑暗的光明?"

寒气噤口,只有时间变化
旅程没有春天——
没有生,没有死,没有时间和太阳
来给你回答。

1926

---

[1] 拉布拉多是加拿大一半岛。

At Melville's Tomb

Often beneath the wave, wide from this ledge
The dice of drowned men's bones he saw bequeath
An embassy. Their numbers as he watched,
Beat on the dusty shore and were obscured.

And wrecks passed without sound of bells,
The calyx of death's bounty giving back
A scattered chapter, livid hieroglyph,
The portent wound in corridors of shells.

Then in the circuit calm of one vast coil,
Its lashings charmed and malice reconciled,
Frosted eyes there were that lifted altars;
And silent answers crept across the stars.

Compass, quadrant and sextant contrive
No farther tides... High in the azure steeps
Monody shall not wake the mariner.
This fabulous shadow only the sea keeps.

1926

在梅尔维尔墓前[1]

经常,在海波下,离暗礁很远,
他看见淹死者的白骨做的骰子
遗下了音信。当他注视,
骰子落在泥岸上,点数模糊。[2]

沉船驶过,没有敲钟,
死亡的猎获物开出花萼送回
断章残简,青黑的象形文字,[3]
贝壳走廊里缠绕着不祥物。

此后,大圆圈中的沉静小圈子,
它的抽击被惑住,解了恨,
迷糊的眼睛高筑起祭坛;
无声的回答爬过星群。

罗盘、四分仪、六分仪,再无法
催起潮水……在蔚蓝的陡岸之上
挽歌无法唤醒水手。
只有大海保存这奇异的影子。

1926

---
1 赫尔曼·梅尔维尔(1819—1891),美国著名作家,《白鲸》的作者,作品大都为海洋小说。
2 据克兰自己解释,这指的是冲上海滩的淹死者的白骨,已经无法辨认是谁的骨头。
3 据克兰自己解释,"花萼"是船沉下时水面的漩涡,"断章残简""象形文字"指漩涡卷起的沉船的散乱物。

Island Quarry

Square sheets—they saw the marble into
Flat slabs there at the marble quarry
At the turning of the road around the roots of the
 mountain
Where the straight road would seem to ply below
 the stone, that fierce
Profile of marble spiked with yonder
Palms against the sunset's towering sea, and maybe
Against mankind. It is at times—

In dusk it is at times as though this island lifted, floated
In Indian baths. At Cuban dusk the eyes
Walking the straight road toward thunder—
This dry road silvering toward the shadow of the
 quarry
—It is at times as though the eyes burned hard and
 glad
And did not take the goat path quivering to the right,
Wide of the mountain—thence to tears and sleep—
But went on into marble that does not weep.

1926

岛上采石场

方石板——他们把大理石
锯成平板,在那山脚
道路转弯处的采石场上
笔直的路好像撬进石缝,那粗暴的
尖矛般的大理石和远处的
手掌一起,插进日暮那高耸的大海,可能
也插进人类世界。在某些时刻——

黄昏就是这种时刻,似乎这岛在升起,漂浮在
印第安温泉上。在古巴的黄昏,眼睛
沿着笔直的路,走向雷电——
这干燥的路银光闪闪,伸向采石场的阴影
——有时候,似乎眼睛被强烈地灼烧,庆幸,
不走上右边那条颤抖的,远远离开大山的,
山羊走的小道——不走向眼泪,不走向睡眠——
而是走进永不哭泣的大理石。

1926

The Bridge

Proem: To Brooklyn Bridge

How many dawns, chill from his rippling rest
The seagull's wings shall dip and pivot him,
Shedding white rings of tumult, building high
Over the chained bay waters Liberty—

Then, with inviolate curve, forsake our eyes
As apparitional as sails that cross
Some page of figures to be filed away;
—Till elevators drop us from our day...

I think of cinemas, panoramic sleights
With multitudes bent toward some flashing scene
Never disclosed, but hastened to again,
Foretold to other eyes on the same screen;

And Thee, across the harbor, silver-paced
As though the sun took step of thee, yet left
Some motion ever unspent in thy stride,—
Implicitly thy freedom staying thee!

桥[1]

序诗：致布鲁克林大桥

多少拂晓，因颤动的休息而受冻，
海鸥的翅膀俯冲忽又旋身向上
洒下骚乱的白环，在被锁住的海湾
海水之上高高地建起自由女神像——

然后，在完美的曲线中，消失
像幻景中的帆一般穿过
几页只待归档的数字；
——直到电梯把我们从白昼降落……

我想到电影，全景的技巧
大群人俯下身来面对闪闪的景色
从未发现真情，却在同一银幕上，
匆匆地向另一些眼睛又做预言；

而你，跨越海湾，银色的步伐
太阳好像跟着你走，你的脚步
却留下一些运动没有使用，——
你的自由暗中把你自己留住！

---

[1] "桥"指纽约的布鲁克林大桥。

Out of some subway scuttle, cell or loft
A bedlamite speeds to thy parapets,
Tilting there momently, shrill shirt ballooning,
A jest falls from the speechless caravan.

Down Wall, from girder into street noon leaks,
A rip-tooth of the sky's acetylene;
All afternoon the cloud-flown derricks turn...
Thy cables breathe the North Atlantic still.

And obscure as that heaven of the Jews,
Thy guerdon... Accolade thou dost bestow
Of anonymity time cannot raise:
Vibrant reprieve and pardon thou dost show.

O harp and altar, of the fury fused,
(How could mere toil align thy choiring strings!)
Terrific threshold of the prophet's pledge,
Prayer of pariah, and the lover's cry,—

Again the traffic lights that skim thy swift
Unfractioned idiom, immaculate sigh of stars,
Beading thy path—condense eternity:
And we have seen night lifted in thine arms.

从地道、小屋或阁楼上跑来

一个疯子高速飞跑冲向栏杆，

一下歪倒，尖叫着衬衣像气球，

一个玩笑从无言的商队里跌落。

正午，从桁梁的空隙漏入街头

像乙炔灯把天空烧裂成齿状；

驾在云头的吊杆整个下午转动……

你的巨缆吹静了北大西洋。

晦暗，就像犹太人的天堂，

你的奖赏……你授予的

无名爵位连时间都无法授予：

你显示了振荡的缓刑和赦免。

哦，狂想熔铸的竖琴和祭坛，

（单靠辛劳怎能调准你合奏的弦！）

先知所预言的可怕的门槛[1]，

漂流者的祈祷，情人的哭泣，——

汽车灯光又掠过你流畅的

不间断的语言，星星洁净的叹息，

珠连起你的路径——凝聚的永恒：

我们看到夜被你的手臂托起。

---

1 圣经中所预言的"地上天堂"的门槛。

Under thy shadow by the piers I waited;
Only in darkness is thy shadow clear.
The City's fiery parcels all undone,
Already snow submerges an iron year...

O Sleepless as the river under thee,
Vaulting the sea, the prairies' dreaming sod,
Unto us lowliest sometime sweep, descend
And of the curveship lend a myth to God.

1930

The Return

The sea raised up a campanile... The wind I heard
Of brine partaking, whirling spout in shower
Of column kiss—that breakers spouted, sheared
Back into bosom—me—her, into natal power...

1933

我在桥墩旁,在你的影子里等待;
在暗处你的影子变得十分清晰。
城市燃烧的包裹全解开了,
白雪已经淹没铁的岁月……

哦,你无眠,就像你身下的水流,
穹盖着大海,和草原做着梦的土地,
有时你猛降到最卑微的我辈身上
用一种曲线性把神话借给上帝。

1930

归来

大海陡立,像钟楼……我听到风
分享咸水,飞旋出圆柱状的吻
像倾盆暴雨——巨浪搏岸,切开
我们的心胸——我——她,切开我们生来就有的
　力量……

1933

伊莉诺·怀利
(Elinor Wylie, 1885-1928)

怀利在20世纪20年代曾蜚声诗坛,是新诗运动中擅长抒情诗的女诗人。

她早年就读于美术学校,但暗中醉心于写诗。她很年轻时就匆忙结婚,不久婚姻关系无法继续,于是跟别人私奔至英国,20世纪20年代回到美国,嫁给诗人威廉·罗斯·倍内。

怀利最早的诗集出版于1912年,均为模仿之作,至1921年她以全部心血写成的诗集《捕风之网》出版,始引起读者注意。她的格律诗技巧娴熟,音律精美,押韵严谨,令人觉得虽丽色迷人,却缺乏热力,似乎像月光下的玉雕,与当时各种以形式创新为目标的新诗运动派别风格迥异,有一种古典美。

1928年的诗集《无聊的呼吸》标志怀利的风格转向成熟,但她不幸早逝于该年12月。

Escape

When foxes eat the last gold grape,
And the last white antelope is killed,
I shall stop fighting and escape
Into a little house I'll build.

But first I'll shrink to fairy size,
With a whisper no one understands,
Making blind moons of all your eyes,
And muddy roads of all your hands.

And you may grope for me in vain
In hollows under the mangrove root,
Or where, in apple-scented rain,
The silver wasp-nests hang like fruit.

1923

潜逃

当狐狸吃完最后的金葡萄,
最后的白羚也被杀戮,
我不再苦斗,我要潜逃,
躲进自造的一间小屋。

我首先缩得小巧玲珑,
把谁也不懂的咒语轻祝,
使你在夜里盲了眼睛,
使你的手变成了泥途。

你在栲树根下洞里摸索,
你找到苹果香味的雨中,
那银蜂的巢,悬挂如水果,
但你永远找不到我的影踪。

1923

Pretty Words

Poets make pets of pretty, docile words:
I love smooth words, like gold-enamelled fish
Which circle slowly with a silken swish,
And tender ones, like downy-feathered birds:
Words shy and dappled, deep-eyed deer in herds,
Come to my hand, and playful if I wish,
Or purring softly at a silver dish,
Blue Persian kittens fed on cream and curds.

I love bright words, words up and singing early;
Words that are luminous in the dark, and sing;
Warm lazy words, white cattle under trees;
I love words opalescent, cool, and pearly,
Like midsummer moths, and honied words like bees,
Gilded and sticky, with a little sting.

1932

可爱的词儿

诗人把可爱、驯良的词视为爱畜:
我爱平滑的词,像上了金釉的鱼,
缓慢地转圈,像丝绸般摆动扭曲,
温和柔弱的词,像有毛茸茸羽毛的鸟:
羞怯有花纹的词,像兽群中黑眼的鹿,
应声而来,而且好玩,驯良温顺,
或者像蓝色的波斯猫朝着银碟,
轻声地咪咪叫,喂的是奶酪凝乳。

我爱明亮的词,一早就飞起歌唱;
在黑暗中唱着歌的词,辉光闪闪;
温暖的懒散的词,树下的白牛犊;
我喜爱珍珠一般的词,乳白、冰凉,
像仲夏夜的流萤,还有的词蜂蜜般甜,
镀着金,长着刺,随时会叫你吃苦。

1932

埃德娜·圣-文森特·米蕾
(Edna St. Vincent Millay, 1892-1950)

米蕾在20世纪二三十年代被认为是最杰出的美国现代女诗人之一。今天在文学史上她的地位没有当初人们设想的那么高,但她的确写出过不少好诗。

据说米蕾五岁就开始写诗。1912年,当她还是个学生时,就发表了名诗《再生》,轰动一时。1923年,她才31岁,就凭诗集《弹竖琴的人》获得刚设立不久的普利策诗歌奖,名满全国。她的诗流畅,技巧纯熟,抒情味很浓,形式整齐,沿用传统格律,内容也多半是传统的诗题:美和爱情。她似乎努力避免使自己的诗带有美国味,而以19世纪英国的浪漫主义诗人为师,她的某些作品的确可以乱真。20世纪20年代初,她关于爱情的十四行诗使她得到了"女拜伦"的美称,但这也可能是她无法发展成一流美国现代诗人的原因。

20世纪20年代,米蕾开始在约翰·里德参与的《解放者》杂志上发表诗歌。这时期她的诗风比较开阔,甚至开始写自由诗,在题材上也比较重视社会内容。

God's World

O world, I cannot hold thee close enough!
    Thy winds, thy wide grey skies!
    Thy mists, that roll and rise!
Thy woods, this autumn day, that ache and sag
And all but cry with colour! That gaunt crag
To crush! To lift the lean of that black bluff!
World, World, I cannot get thee close enough!

Long have I known a glory in it all,
    But never knew I this;
    Here such a passion is
As stretcheth me apart,—Lord, I do fear
Thou'st made the world too beautiful this year;
My soul is all but out of me,—let fall
No burning leaf; prithee, let no bird call.

                            1917

上帝的世界

哦世界,我多想把你抱得更紧!
  你的风,你灰色的长空!
  你的雾,翻卷,升腾!
这秋日,你的树林,疼痛地下垂
差点哭掉颜色!这巉岩憔悴
就要压碎!就要抬起倾斜的黑色陡峰!
世界,世界,我多想把你抱得更紧!

我早就看到过最壮丽的景色,
    但从未见如此美景;
    饱含着如此深情
差点把我撕碎,——上帝,我惊骇
今年您把世界变得实在太美;
使我心摇魂销,——哦您别让
燃烧的叶子飘飞;请,别让鸟唱。

1917

"What Lips My Lips Have Kissed, and Where, and Why"

What lips my lips have kissed, and where, and why,
I have forgotten, and what arms have lain
Under my head till morning; but the rain
Is full of ghosts tonight, that tap and sigh
Upon the glass and listen for reply,
And in my heart there stirs a quiet pain
For unremembered lads that not again
Will turn to me at midnight with a cry.

Thus in winter stands the lonely tree,
Nor knows what birds have vanished one by one,
Yet knows its boughs more silent than before:
I cannot say what loves have come and gone,
I only know that summer sang in me
A little while, that in me sings no more.

1923

"我的唇吻过谁的唇,在哪里,为什么"

我的唇吻过谁的唇,在哪里,为什么,
我已忘记,谁的手臂
我枕着直到天明;但今夜雨水
满是鬼魂,敲打着窗子玻璃
唉声叹气,倾听着我的回音,
我心中翻滚着安详的痛苦
因为早已忘却的少年再不会
在午夜转身朝着我喊我一声。

孤独的树站立在冬寒之中,
它不知是什么鸟一只只消失,
只知树枝比从前更加冷清:
我说不出什么爱情来了又去,
只知道夏季在我心中唱过
一阵子,现在只剩一片寂静。

1923

The Goose-girl

Spring rides no horses down the hill,
But comes on foot, a goose-girl still.
And all the loveliest things there be
Come simply, so, it seems to me.
If ever I said, in grief or pride,
I tired of honest things, I lied:
And should be cursed forevermore
With Love in laces, like a whore,
And neighbours cold, and friends unsteady,
And Spring on horseback, like a lady!

1923

Never May the Fruit Be Plucked

Never, never may the fruit be plucked from the bough
And gathered into barrels.
He that would eat of love must eat it where it hangs.
Though the branches bend like reeds,
Though the ripe fruit splash in the grass or wrinkle
  on the tree,
He that would eat of love may bear away with him

养鹅姑娘

春天不是骑马走下山岗,
她步行,依旧是养鹅姑娘。
所有最最可爱的事物
依我看,都,来得朴素。
若我得意或伤心过度,竟然说
我厌倦了诚实,那是胡扯:
我将永远受诅咒,
爱情像妓女,遍体绫绸,
邻居如陌路,友人多反复,
春天骑马而来,有如贵妇!

1923

永远别摘果子

永远,永远别从枝上摘下果子
收进桶里。
那些想品尝爱情的人,必须就地品尝。
虽然树枝曲如芦苇,
虽然熟果在草上跌破,在树上皱缩,
想品尝爱情的人,只能带走

Only what his belly can hold,

Nothing in the apron,

Nothing in the pockets.

Never, never may the fruit be gathered from the
    bough

And harvested in barrels.

The winter of love is a cellar of empty bins,

In an orchard soft with rot.

1923

Wild Swans

I looked in my heart while the wild swans went over.

And what did I see I had not seen before?

Only a question less or a question more;

Nothing to match the flight of wild birds flying.

Tiresome heart, forever living and dying,

House without air, I leave you and lock your door.

Wild swans, come over the town, come over

The town again, trailing your legs and crying!

1923

他肚子能盛下的东西,
不准围裙兜,
不准口袋装。
永远,永远别从枝上摘下果子
收进桶里。
爱情的冬天,是满地腐叶败果的花园里,
一个地窖,堆着空的箱篓。

        1923

野天鹅

当野天鹅飞过,我注视内心。
能见到什么新的东西?
只是多一个或少一个问题;
根本比不上野天鹅的飞行。
疲倦的心,永远死死生生,
不透气的屋子,我离开、锁起。
野天鹅,来啊,再一次
飞过城市,曳着后腿,长声唳鸣!

        1923

For Pao-chin, a Boatman on the Yellow Sea

Where is he now, in his soiled shirt reeking of garlic,
Sculling his sampan home, and night approaching
    fast—
The red sail hanging wrinkled on the bamboo mast;
Where is he now, I shall remember my whole life long
With love and praise, for the sake of a small song
Played on a Chinese flute?
I have been sad;
I have been in cities where the song was all I had,—
A treasure never to be bartered by the hungry days.

Where is he now, for whom I carry in my heart
This love, this praise?

                                       1928

致黄海船夫鲍金[1]

此刻他在何方?脏衬衣有大蒜味,
划着舢板回家,夜色匆忙——
红色的帆皱缩在竹桅杆上;
此刻他在何方?我一生将永远记住
带着爱,带着赞美,为了那支小曲
在中国横笛上奏出。
我悲伤过;
困居在市嚣中,只剩这支歌,——
再挨饿我也不会把它出卖。

此刻他在何方?我心中把他思念
带着爱,带着赞美。

1928

---

[1] 鲍金,音译。米蕾曾到访中国,去过山东芝罘。

Justice Denied in Massachusetts

Let us abandon then our gardens and go home
And sit in the sitting-room
Shall the larkspur blossom or the corn grow under
 this cloud?
Sour to the fruitful seed
Is the cold earth under this cloud,
Fostering quack and weed, we have marched upon
 but cannot conquer;
We have bent the blades of our hoes against the
 stalks of them.

Let us go home, and sit in the sitting-room.
Not in our day
Shall the cloud go over and the sun rise as before,
Beneficent upon us
Out of the glittering bay,
And the warm winds be blown inward from the sea
Moving the blades of corn
With a peaceful sound.

Forlorn, forlorn,
Stands the blue hay-rack by the empty mow.
And the petals drop to the ground,

在马萨诸塞正义被拒绝[1]

让我们离开花园回家吧

静静地坐在房间里。

如此阴云下,飞燕花和玉米能生长吗?

这阴云下冰凉的土地

一直酸到水果的种子里,

只能培育骗子和莠草,我们进军了,但没能
　胜利;

为除掉这些草,我们砍弯了锄头。

让我们回家吧,静静地坐着。

在我们今日

乌云不会廓清,太阳不会如往昔

从那闪烁的海湾升起

给我们以光明,

温暖的风也不会从海上吹进来

摇动玉米叶子

发出安宁的沙沙声。

被抛弃了,被抛弃了,

那蓝色的草垛站在空空草场旁。

花瓣坠落到地上,

---

[1] 1927年,美国工人运动的两个积极分子萨科和瓦内蒂被误判死刑,美国进步人士曾和工人群众一齐为此案进行了艰苦地斗争,但都没有成功。这首诗是米蕾在两位烈士行刑前写成的。

Leaving the tree unfruited.
The sun that warmed our stooping backs and withered
    the weed uprooted—
We shall not feel it again.
We shall die in darkness, and be buried in the rain.

What from the splendid dead
We have inherited—
Furrows sweet to the grain, and the weed subdued—
See now the slug and the mildew plunder.
Evil does overwhelm
The larkspur and the corn;
We have seen them go under.

Let us sit here, sit still,
Here in the sitting-room until we die;
At the step of Death on the walk, rise and go;
Leaving to our children's children the beautiful doorway,
And this elm,
And a blighted earth to till
With a broken hoe.

1928

使树结不出果。
太阳曾晒暖我们弯下的背脊,使拔起的莠草
 枯萎——
我们再也感受不到太阳。
我们将死在黑暗里,在阴雨中被埋葬。

从那两个光荣的死者身上
我们继承了什么——
适合谷物生长的田垄,莠草除尽——
而如今瞧这些渣滓和发霉的赃物。
罪恶压垮了
飞燕花和玉米;
我们看到他们倒下。

让我们坐在这儿,静静地坐着,
坐在房间里,等待死亡;
当死神的脚步声传来,就站起来走吧;
给我们孩子的孩子留下这美丽的门廊,
还有这榆树,
这被蹂躏的有待耕耘的土地
这破裂的锄。

1928

On Hearing a Symphony of Beethoven

Sweet sounds, oh, beautiful music, do not cease!

Reject me not into the world again.

With you alone is excellence and peace,

Mankind made plausible, his purpose plain.

Enchanted in your air benign and shrewd,

With limbs a-sprawl and empty faces pale,

The spiteful and the stingy and the rude

Sleep like the scullions in the fairy-tale.

This moment is the best the world can give:

The tranquil blossom on the tortured stem.

Reject me not, sweet sounds; oh, let me live,

Till Doom espy my towers and scatter them,

A city spell-bound under the aging sun.

Music my rampart, and my only one.

                                    1928

听贝多芬的交响乐

可爱的声音,哦,美丽的音乐,别停!
别拒绝我,别把我重新抛入尘世。
只有在你这儿有优美,有安宁,
人类充满信心,目标显得分明。
那些可鄙、吝啬、粗蠢的家伙,
四肢摊开,空虚的脸变得苍白,
被你的慈爱精美的曲调着了魔,
就像童话中的奴仆一样安睡。
这是人世所能有的最美的时刻:
是雨摧风折的枝干上宁静的花卉。
别抛弃我,可爱的声音;哦,让我活,
直到末日找到我的塔楼,把它们摧毁,
衰老的太阳下这符咒镇住的城市。
音乐是我的堡垒,我唯一的工事。

1928

For You There Is No Song

For you there is no song...
> Only the shaking

Of the voice that meant to sing; the sound of the strong
> Voice breaking.

Strange in my hand appears
> The pen, and yours broken.

There are ink and tears on the page; only the tears
> Have spoken.

1928

悼歌[1]

没有歌献给您……
    只有声声颤动
发自原准备唱歌的喉咙；那坚强的喉咙
    破裂的声音。

多奇怪,这笔在我手里
    出现,而你的笔破碎。
纸上有墨有泪;而说话的
    只是泪水。

            1928

---

[1] 1928年女诗人怀利不幸早逝,米蕾写了一组悼诗,这是其中的第二首。

克劳德·麦开
(Claude McKay, 1889-1948)

20世纪20年代至30年代初，以纽约的黑人聚居区哈莱姆为中心，出现了现代美国黑人文学艺术的第一次高潮，史称"哈莱姆文艺复兴"。克劳德·麦开是哈莱姆文艺复兴的先驱人物。

麦开出生于加勒比地区牙买加的一个黑人农民家庭，曾做过木匠和警察等职，1912年出版了以牙买加的英语写的诗集《牙买加之歌》，描写牙买加山区的风光和农家生活。同年，他到美国求学，但不久就移居哈莱姆区，一边写诗，一边靠当饭店侍者为生。起先他仍用牙买加方言写作，后来他渐渐抛弃这种方式（即19世纪一些黑人诗人创作诗歌时依靠方言俚语取得独特的色彩），而采用标准的英语和传统的格律诗形式进行创作。1920年出版的《新罕布什尔之春》，尤其是1922年的诗集《哈莱姆的孤影》，唱出了美国大城市中黑人群众的痛苦、愤怒和反抗的意志，受到热烈欢迎。

1921年起，麦开参与编辑了美国共产党领导的刊物《群众》和《解放者》，1923年到苏联，会见了列宁，并作为美国工人党代表参加第三国际工作。

20世纪20年代后期，麦开脱离了政治活动，停止诗歌创作，思想渐渐消沉。他晚年成为天主教徒，并在天主教小学教书，在贫困中终其一生。

麦开是现代美国第一个以现实主义的方式来反映黑人在城市劳苦生活的黑人诗人。他启迪了整整一代黑人诗人，因此在美国黑人文学史上他的贡献始终被人牢记。

Spring in New Hampshire

Too green the springing April grass,
    Too blue the silver-speckled sky,
For me to linger here, alas,
    While happy winds go laughing by,
Wasting the golden hours indoors,
Washing windows and scrubbing floors.

Too wonderful the April night,
    Too faintly sweet the first May flowers,
The stars too gloriously bright,
    For me to spend the evening hours,
When fields are fresh and streams are leaping,
Wearied, exhausted, dully sleeping.

1920

If We Must Die

If we must die, let it not be like hogs
Hunted and penned in an inglorious spot,

新罕布什尔之春

太绿了,这四月芳草蓊蔚,
　　太蓝了,这晴空银光闪烁,
叫我怎么留在屋内,唉,
　　当快乐的风大笑着飞过,
黄金的日子在户内荒废,
窗子要擦,地板要抹。

这四月之夜真太奇美,
　　这五月的早花香味清淡,
太明亮了,这星星的光辉,
　　如此良夜,叫我怎么办?
当平野铺绣,流溪溅翠,
而我精疲力尽,昏昏入睡。

　　　　　　　　　　　1920

哪怕我们必死 [1]

哪怕我们必死,也别死得像猪
被兜捕然后关入肮脏的栏圈,

---

[1] 这是麦开最为人传诵的一首诗,曾被丘吉尔在英国议会报告时引用,成为反法西斯的战斗口号。但麦开最初写此诗是为纪念1919年黑人暴动。

While round us bark the mad and hungry dogs,

Making their mock at our accursèd lot.

If we must die, O let us nobly die,

So that our precious blood may not be shed

In vain; then even the monsters we defy

Shall be constrained to honor us though dead!

O kinsmen! we must meet the common foe!

Though far outnumbered let us show us brave,

And for their thousand blows deal one death-blow!

What though before us lies the open grave?

Like men we'll face the murderous, cowardly pack,

Pressed to the wall, dying, but fighting back!

1920

America

Although she feeds me bread of bitterness,

And sinks into my throat her tiger's tooth,

Stealing my breath of life, I will confess

I love this cultured hell that tests my youth!

Her vigor flows like tides into my blood,

Giving me strength erect against her hate.

Her bigness sweeps my being like a flood.

疯狂的饿狗围着我们乱吠狂呼,
把我们悲剧的命运当作笑谈。
哪怕我们必死,也要死得高贵,
这样我们宝贵的血就不至于
白白流失;甚至我们抵抗的恶鬼
也得被迫对我们的死表示敬意!
哦同胞们! 我们必须共同抗敌!
尽管众寡悬殊,也要现出勇气,
挨打千次,也要回敬致命的一击!
即使面前是敞开的坟墓又有何关系!
面对残暴又胆怯的匪徒,像男子汉,
退到墙根,即将死去,也继续作战!

1920

美国

尽管她给我的面包满嘴苦涩,
把虎牙直咬进我的咽喉里,
偷走了我的呼吸,我还得说,
我爱这考验青春的文明地狱!
她的朝气流入我的血一如巨潮,
给我力量昂然面对她的仇恨。
她的广袤如洪水把我横扫。

Yet, as a rebel fronts a king in state,
I stand within her walls with not a shred
Of terror, malice, not a word of jeer.
Darkly I gaze into the days ahead,
And see her might and granite wonders there,
Beneath the touch of Time's unerring hand,
Like priceless treasures sinking in the sand.

1922

Harlem Shadows

I hear the halting footsteps of a lass
    In Negro Harlem when the night lets fall
Its veil. I see the shapes of girls who pass
    To bend and barter at desire's call.
Ah, little dark girls who in slippered feet
Go prowling through the night from street to street!

Through the long night until the silver break
    Of day the little gray feet know no rest;
Through the lone night until the last snow-flake
    Has dropped from heaven upon the earth's white
        breast,

然而,像叛逆者面对暴君
我站在她墙内,没有一丝
恐惧、怨恨,也没一字讥议。
阴暗地,我注视着前面的日子,
看到她的伟力,花岗岩的奇迹,
在时间准确无误的手掌触摸之下,
就好像无价之宝沉入黄沙。

1922

哈莱姆的孤影

我听到一个姑娘脚步逡巡
　　在黑人区哈莱姆,当沉沉黑夜
放下面纱。我看见姑娘们飘过的身影
　　向欲望的要求屈膝交易。
啊,娇小的黑姑娘,穿拖鞋的脚
整夜徘徊,一条街,接着一条!

长夜漫漫,直到银色清晓
　　那灰暗的小脚永不止步;
长夜漫漫,直到最后一片雪
　　落到大地白色的胸脯,

The dusky, half-clad girls of tired feet
Are trudging, thinly shod, from street to street.

Ah, stern harsh world, that in the wretched way
  Of poverty, dishonor and disgrace,
Has pushed the timid little feet of clay,
  The sacred brown feet of my fallen race!
Ah, heart of me, the weary, weary feet
In Harlem wandering from street to street.

1922

黑姑娘衣履单薄，疲倦的脚
无力地踯躅，一条街，接着一条。

啊，冷酷的世界，如此卑鄙
  用贫困，侮慢，羞辱和欺凌，
把这胆怯的泥脚催逼，
  我沦落种族的脚，棕黑，神圣！
啊，我的心，这疲倦，疲倦的脚
在哈莱姆流浪，一条街，接着一条。

1922

康梯·喀伦
(Countee Cullen, 1903—1946)

喀伦是哈莱姆文艺复兴的代表人物之一。他成长在一个黑人牧师家庭，受过良好教育，在中学时代就是许多诗歌比赛的得奖者。1925年，在纽约大学获得学士学位；1926年，在哈佛大学获得硕士学位；1928年与著名黑人学者杜波依斯的女儿结婚（后离异），此后一直在纽约做中学教师。

1925年在纽约大学读书时，喀伦出版诗集《颜色》；1927年出版的《黄铜太阳》和《棕色女郎之歌》使他诗名大盛；1929年出版的《黑基督》是他最出色的作品。此外，他还曾经参与编辑著名的黑人刊物《机会》。

喀伦写的大都是格律诗，形式严整。他对种族压迫的抗议是温和的，是一种有克制的义愤，代表了黑人诗歌运动一派的诗风。20世纪30年代后，他写过一部长篇小说，但诗作很少。遗作于1947年辑成《我坚持》出版。

Incident

Once riding in old Baltimore,
    Heart-filled, head-filled with glee,
I saw a Baltimorean
    Keep looking straight at me.

Now I was eight and very small,
    And he was no whit bigger,
And so I smiled, but he poked out
    His tongue, and called me, "Nigger."

I saw the whole of Baltimore
    From May until December;
Of all the things that happened there
    That's all that I remember.

                        1925

For a Lady I Know

She even thinks that up in heaven
Her class lies late and snores,
While poor black cherubs rise at seven
To do celestial chores.

                        1925

一桩事情

我坐车上巴尔的摩老城,
　　满心快乐,满脑快活,
我看到一个巴尔的摩人
　　目不转睛向我瞅着。

那时我很小,才只有八岁,
　　他是跟我一般大的小孩,
所以我微笑,而他吐出
　　舌头,叫我"黑鬼"。

我玩遍了巴尔的摩,
　　从五月玩到年底;
那里的事我全忘了
　　只有这桩老记在心里。

　　　　　　　　　1925

为一个我认识的夫人代书

　　她认为哪怕上在天堂
　　她那阶级高卧迟迟,
　　而穷苦的黑天童七点起身
　　做天上的杂事粗活。

　　　　　　　　　1925

From the Dark Tower

We shall not always plant while others reap

The golden increment of bursting fruit,

Not always countenance, abject and mute,

That lesser men should hold their brothers cheap;

Not everlastingly while others sleep

Shall we beguile their limbs with mellow flute,

Not always bend to some more subtle brute;

We were not made to eternally weep.

The night whose sable breast relieves the stark,

White stars is no less lovely being dark,

And there are buds that cannot bloom at all

In light, but crumple, piteous, and fall;

So in the dark we hide the heart that bleeds,

And wait, and tend our agonizing seeds.

1927

从黑塔上

不会永远是我们种，别人收获

那熟透的果子黄金般的利润，

不会永远带着沮丧、沉默的面容，

让卑劣的小人轻视他们的大哥；

不会永远让别人高卧，我们自己

吹起悠扬的笛声让他们躺得安乐，

不会永远向狡狯的禽兽俯首；

我们不是命中注定永远哭泣。

夜，赤裸的白星在黑色的胸前

更加耀眼，它黑却更秀妍，

有的蓓蕾在白昼不会开花，

蜷缩枯萎，惨惨戚戚地跌下；

在黑暗里，我们把滴血的心藏起，

等待，并且培育苦苦挣扎的种子。

1927

简·吐默
(Jean Toomer, 1894-1967)

吐默是哈莱姆文艺复兴的另一位重要诗人。但他除有黑人血统外,还有法、荷、德、意、犹太、印第安等血统,他可以混在白人中,但他宁愿宣称自己是个黑人,因为他认为黑人反种族歧视和压迫的斗争是正义的。

他兴趣多样,分别在不同学院攻读过体育生物学、社会学、历史等专业,后来他做了一名教师。1922年,进步刊物《解放者》开始发表他的作品;1923年,他出版了著名诗、文、剧本混编的集子《甘蔗》,这也是哈莱姆文艺复兴取得的一个重要成绩。

奇怪的是,这位天才的黑人作家仅昙花一现。《甘蔗》问世后,他就从文坛上消失了,他的兴趣转向心理学和神秘主义。他两次娶富家白人女儿为妻,甚至不再承认自己是黑人。他偶尔也写文学作品,但这些作品已失去文学价值,无人肯出版,直到他死去还是一堆手稿。

Song of the Son

Pour, O pour that parting soul in song,
O pour it in the saw-dust glow of night,
Into the velvet pine-smoke air tonight,
And let the valley carry it along.
And let the valley carry it along.

O land and soil, red soil and sweet-gum tree
So scant of grass, so profligate of pines,
Now just before an epoch's sun declines
Thy son, in time, I have returned to thee,
Thy son, I have in time returned to thee.

In time, for though the sun is setting on
A song-lit race of slaves, it has not set;
Though late, O soil, it is not too late yet
To catch thy plaintive soul, leaving, soon gone,
Leaving, to catch thy plaintive soul soon gone.

O Negro slaves, dark purple ripened plums,
Squeezed, and bursting in the pine-wood air,
Passing, before they stripped the old tree bare
One plum was saved for me, one seed becomes

儿子的歌

倾吐，哦往歌中倾吐离情，
哦，倾入木屑般燃红的夜里，
带着天鹅绒般的松烟气息，
让山谷带走歌声。
让山谷带走歌声。

哦大地，甜胶树，红色的大地，
青草稀疏，但是青松茂美，
正当时代的太阳即将倾颓
我，你的儿子，赶上回来见你。
你的儿子，我，赶上回来见你。

正赶上，在这善歌的奴隶种族头顶
太阳虽已下沉，但却没有消失；
虽然晚了，哦大地，还来得及
追上你一去不返的，悲伤的，灵魂，
追上你悲伤的一去不返的灵魂。

哦黑奴，紫黑色熟透的梅子，
受压榨，破裂时发出松树香气，
逝去，趁他们未把这老树剥皮
留下了一颗梅子给我，一颗种子

An everlasting song, a singing tree,
Caroling softly souls of slavery,
What they were, and what they are to me,
Caroling softly souls of slavery.

1923

Harvest Song

I am a reaper whose muscles set at sundown. All my oats are cradled.
But I am too chilled, and too fatigued to bind them. And I hunger.

I crack a grain between my teeth. I do not taste it.
I have been in the fields all day. My throat is dry. I hunger.

My eyes are caked with dust of oatfields at harvest-time.
I am a blind man who stares across the hills, seeking stack'd fields of other harvesters.

变成一首永恒的歌,一棵唱歌的树,
柔和地咏唱黑奴的灵魂,
对我唱过去,对我唱现在,
柔和地咏唱黑奴的灵魂。

1923

收割歌

我是个割麦人,日落时我浑身筋肉麻痹。所有的
  燕麦已全割完。
但我太冷、太累,没力气捆麦。我饿。

我咬碎一颗麦粒。我尝不出滋味。
我在田里已一整天。喉干舌燥。我饿。

两眼被收获季节麦田的尘土糊住了。
我是个瞎子,瞪视着山那边,在堆着麦垛的田间找
  其他割麦人。

It would be good to see them... crook'd, split, and iron-ring'd handles of the scythes. It would be good to see them, dust-caked and blind. I hunger.

(Dusk is a strange fear'd sheath their blades are dull'd in.)
My throat is dry. And should I call, a cracked grain like the oats... eoho—

I fear to call. What should they hear me, and offer me their grain, oats, or wheat or corn? I have been in the fields all day. I fear I could not taste it. I fear knowledge of my hunger.

My ears are caked with dust of oatfields at harvest-time.
I am a deaf man who strains to hear the calls of other harvesters whose throats are also dry.

It would be good to hear their songs... reapers of the sweet-stalk'd cane, cutters of the corn... even though their throats cracked and the strangeness of their voices deafened me.

能见到他们有多好……见到弯曲的、坼裂的、带铁环的镰刀柄。哪怕见到他们两眼被灰糊住成了瞎子也好。我饿。

(夜色是剑鞘把那奇特的恐怖刀锋给藏起来。)
我的咽喉干燥。当我喊叫,里面有一颗燕麦似的坼裂的肿块……依噢嗬——

我怕叫喊。要是他们听到我,过来给我吃他们的谷粒、燕麦、麦子、玉米怎么办?我在田里一整天。我怕我已尝不出滋味。我怕饥饿的滋味。

我的耳朵被收获季节麦田里的灰尘糊住了。
我是聋子,我拼命想听见其他割麦人的叫喊,但他们的喉咙也干了。

能听见他们的歌声有多好……那些甜茎甘蔗的收割者,那些玉米的收割者……哪怕他们的嗓子也坼裂了,哪怕他们的声音太奇怪会把我吓聋。

I hunger. My throat is dry. Now that the sun has set and I am chilled, I fear to call. (Eoho, my brothers!)

I am a reaper, (Eoho!) All my oats are cradled. But I am too fatigued to bind them. And I hunger. I crack a grain. It has no taste to it. My throat is dry...

O my brothers, I beat my palms, still soft, against the stubble of my harvesting. (You beat your soft palms, too.) My pain is sweet. Sweeter than the oats or wheat or corn. It will not bring me knowledge of my hunger.

1923

Her Lips Are Copper Wire

    whisper of yellow globes
    gleaming on lamp-posts that sway
    like bootleg licker drinkers in the fog

    and let your breath be moist against me
    like bright beads on yellow globes

我饿。我喉咙干了。太阳全部落下,我冷。我怕叫喊。(依噢嗬,弟兄们!)

我是个割麦人,(依噢嗬!)我的麦已全割完。但我太累了,没力气捆。我饿。我咬碎一颗麦。我尝不出滋味。我的喉咙已干……

哦,弟兄们,我轻轻用手掌,拍麦茬。(你也轻轻用手掌拍麦茬吧。)这疼痛是甜蜜的。比燕麦甜,比麦子甜,比玉米甜。疼痛能使我忘却饥饿的滋味。

1923

她的嘴唇是电线

摇摇晃晃的路灯杆上
黄灯泡低声细语
好像雾中一批醉汉

让你对着我的呼吸也潮湿
像黄灯泡上发亮的水珠

telephone the power-house

that the main wires are insulate

(her words play softly up and down

dewy corridors of billboards)

then with your tongue remove the tape

and press your lips to mine

till they are incandescent

1923

打电话给发电厂

就说主线是绝缘的

(她的话语温柔地起伏

露水沾湿的广告牌走廊)

然后,用你的舌头拆掉胶布

把你嘴唇紧压在我的唇上

直到它们发出白炽的光

1923

兰斯敦·休斯
(Langston Hughes, 1902-1967)

休斯是现代美国最优秀的黑人诗人之一，被称为"哈莱姆的桂冠诗人"。他的自由诗开阔、舒展、节奏热情，像爵士乐那样强烈。他的很多诗被谱成曲，他自己也是个出色的诗歌朗诵家。

休斯在中学时就开始写诗。他父亲在墨西哥经商发迹，想让他成为工程师，但他在哥伦比亚大学只读了一年就离开了，之后远行非洲、欧洲，回国后在华盛顿一餐厅做侍者。据说有一天，正好著名诗人伐切尔·林赛到这里用餐，休斯不敢直接找林赛，而把几首自己的诗压在林赛的盘子下，林赛立即发现这些诗的节奏之美，向全厅朗读，休斯由此一举成名。

1926年休斯出版著名的诗集《疲倦的布鲁斯》，1930年出版长篇小说《不是没有笑》，都成为哈莱姆文艺复兴的名著。20世纪30年代他到过苏联、中国和内战中的西班牙，写了不少支持各国人民斗争的诗歌，尤其对中国的革命斗争表现了很高热情。他的后期作品多为小说，他创造了一个黑人工人形象森普尔，以此为主角写了一系列作品来描写黑人小市民的生活情态。

休斯的作品之所以至今仍赢得人们的赞赏，是由于他的诗境界比较开阔。他从黑人的痛苦和憧憬中获取内容，而且他把黑人的形象与整个人类文明史上的奴隶形象联系起来，这样就给予他的诗以更深远的意义和更震动人心的力量。他从黑人的音乐和民歌中汲取营养，把爵士乐的节奏融入于自由诗之中，在这些方面，他与桑德堡颇为相似。休斯的创作，对于美国现代黑人文学的发展，甚至对非洲黑人国家文学的觉醒，都有重大影响。

The Negro

I am a Negro:
> Black as the night is black,
> Black like the depths of my Africa.

I've been a slave:
> Caesar told me to keep his door-steps clean.
> I brushed the boots of Washington.

I've been a worker:
> Under my hand the pyramids arose.
> I made mortar for the Woolworth Building.

I've been a singer:
> All the way from Africa to Georgia
> I carried my sorrow songs.
> I made ragtime.

I've been a victim:
> The Belgians cut off my hands in the Congo.
> They lynch me still in Mississippi.

黑人[1]

我是黑人：

　　像黑夜一样黑，

　　像我的非洲腹地一样黑。

我是奴隶：

　　凯撒要我洗大门。

　　华盛顿让我擦靴子。

我是工人：

　　金字塔在我手下升起。

　　我给伍尔沃思大楼[2]拌灰泥。

我是歌手：

　　打非洲来到佐治亚

　　一路带来悲伤的歌。

　　我演出爵士乐。

我是牺牲者：

　　比利时人在刚果剁断我的手。

　　现在我在密西西比受私刑。

1　此诗是诗集《疲倦的布鲁斯》之序诗。
2　纽约一座著名的摩天大楼。

I am a Negro:

    Black as the night is black,

    Black like the depths of my Africa.

1926

The Negro Speaks of Rivers

I've known rivers:
I've known rivers ancient as the world and older
   than the flow of human blood in human veins.

My soul has grown deep like the rivers.

I bathed in the Euphrates when dawns were young.
I built my hut near the Congo and it lulled me to
   sleep.
I looked upon the Nile and raised the pyramids
   above it.
I heard the singing of the Mississippi when Abe
   Lincoln went down to New Orleans, and I've seen
   its muddy bosom turn all golden in the sunset.

我是黑人:

　　像黑夜一样黑,

　　像我的非洲腹地一样黑。

1926

黑人谈河

我了解河流:
我了解的河流和世界一样古老,比人类血管中的血
　流还要古老。

我的灵魂与河流一样深沉。

当朝霞初升,我沐浴在幼发拉底河。
我在刚果河旁搭茅棚,波声催我入睡。
我俯视着尼罗河,建起了金字塔。
当阿伯[1]·林肯南下新奥尔良,我听到密西西比河在歌
　唱,我看到河流混浊的胸脯被落日染得一江金黄。

---

[1] 阿伯是阿伯拉罕这名字的简称,又译亚伯拉罕。

I've known rivers:

Ancient, dusky rivers.

My soul has grown deep like the rivers.

1926

As I Grew Older

It was a long time ago.

I have almost forgotten my dream.

But it was there then,

In front of me,

Bright like a sun—

My dream.

And then the wall rose,

Rose slowly,

Slowly,

Between me and my dream.

Rose slowly, slowly,

Dimming,

Hiding,

The light of my dream.

我了解河流:

古老的,幽暗的河流。

我的灵魂与河流一样深沉。

1926

我长大了

那还是多年以前。
我几乎忘掉了我的梦。
但以前我有过,
在我眼前,
辉煌如太阳——
是我的梦。

后来,那墙升起,
慢慢升起,
慢慢地,
把我和我的梦隔开。
慢慢升起,慢慢地,
遮暗了,
盖住了,
我那梦的光辉。

Rose until it touched the sky—
The wall.

Shadow.
I am black.

I lie down in the shadow.
No longer the light of my dream before me,
Above me.
Only the thick wall.
Only the shadow.

My hands!
My dark hands!
Break through the wall!
Find my dream!
Help me to shatter this darkness,
To smash this night,
To break this shadow
Into a thousand lights of sun,
Into a thousand whirling dreams
Of sun!

1926

升起,直到碰上天——

这墙。

这阴影。

我是黑的。

我躺在阴影里。

再没有梦的光辉照在我面前,

照在我头顶。

只有厚厚的墙。

只有阴影。

我的手!

我黑色的手!

快打破墙!

快找回我的梦!

帮我打碎这黑暗,

摧毁这暗夜,

击破这阴影

把它变成千柱阳光,

变成一千个飞旋的梦

梦到太阳!

1926

I, Too

I, too, sing America.

I am the darker brother.
They send me to eat in the kitchen
When company comes,
But I laugh,
And eat well,
And grow strong.

Tomorrow,
I'll be at the table
When company comes.
Nobody'll dare
Say to me,
"Eat in the kitchen,"
Then.

Besides,
They'll see how beautiful I am
And be ashamed—

I, too, am America.

1926

我,也来[1]

我,也来,歌唱美国。

在弟兄中,我肤色深些。
有客来时
他们打发我上厨房去吃,
可是我大笑,
我吃得很香,
长得结实。

明天,
有客来时
我要坐在桌旁。
那时,
谁也不敢
对我嚷嚷:
"上厨房去吃。"

而且,
他们会看到我多么美
他们要自惭形秽——

我,也是,美国。

1926

---

[1] 标题套自惠特曼的名诗《我歌唱美国》,此诗是《疲倦的布鲁斯》的尾声。

Brass Spittoons

Clean the spittoons, boy.
>   Detroit,
>   Chicago,
>   Atlantic City,
>   Palm Beach.

Clean the spittoons.
The steam in hotel kitchens,
And the smoke in hotel lobbies,
And the slime in hotel spittoons:
Part of my life.
>   Hey, boy!
>   A nickel,
>   A dime,
>   A dollar,

Two dollars a day.
>   Hey, boy!
>   A nickel,
>   A dime,
>   A dollar,
>   Two dollars

Buy shoes for the baby.
House rent to pay.
Gin on Saturday,

铜痰盂

擦痰盂,堂倌。

　　底特律,

　　芝加哥,

　　大西洋城,

　　棕榈滩。

擦痰盂。

旅馆厨房的蒸汽,

旅馆门廊的烟雾,

旅馆痰盂的腌臜:

是我生命的一部分。

　　嗨,堂倌!

　　一文钱,

　　一毛钱,

　　一元钱,

两元钱一天。

　　嗨,堂倌!

　　一文钱,

　　一毛钱,

　　一元钱,

　　两元钱

给孩子买鞋。

付房租。

星期六杜松子酒,

Church on Sunday.

    My God!

Babies and gin and church

And women and Sunday

All mixed with dimes and

Dollars and clean spittoons

And house rent to pay.

    Hey, boy!

A bright bowl of brass is beautiful to the Lord.

Bright polished brass like the cymbals

Of King David's dancers,

Like the wine cups of Solomon.

    Hey, boy!

A clean spittoon on the altar of the Lord.

A clean bright spittoon all newly polished,—

At least I can offer that.

    Com'mere, boy!

                                        1927

星期天上教堂。

　　我的上帝!

小孩,酒,教堂,

还有女人,还有星期天

全混起来了,硬币

美元,擦亮的痰盂,

还有要付的房钱。

　　嗨,堂倌!

闪光的铜痰盂上帝见了也喜欢。

擦亮的铜痰盂就像是

大卫王舞伎手里的铙钹,

所罗门王手里的金盏。

　　嗨,堂倌!

擦亮的痰盂供上我主的祭坛,

才擦好的光亮的痰盂,——

至少我能把这贡献。

　　来啊,堂倌!

1927

Song for a Dark Girl

Way Down South in Dixie
    (Break the heart of me)
They hung my black young lover
    To a cross roads tree.

Way Down South in Dixie
    (Bruised body high in air)
I asked the white Lord Jesus
    What was the use of prayer.

Way Down South in Dixie
    (Break the heart of me)
Love is a naked shadow
    On a gnarled and naked tree.

                1927

Merry-go-round

Colored child at carnival:

为一个黑姑娘唱的歌

在南方,在迪克西[1]
　　(我的心裂成碎片)
他们把我的黑情郎
　　吊在路口的树上。

在南方,在迪克西
　　(打烂的身体高挂空中)
我问白皮肤耶稣我主
　　祈祷还有什么用。

在南方,在迪克西,
　　(我的心裂成碎片)
爱情成了赤裸的黑影
　　吊在赤裸多节的树上。

1927

回转木马

　　　狂欢节的黑孩子:

1　南部各州的俗称。

Where is the Jim Crow section
On this merry-go-round,
Mister, 'cause I want to ride?
Down South where I come from
White and colored
Can't sit side by side.
Down South on the train
There's a Jim Crow car.
On the bus we're put in the back—
But there ain't no back
To a merry-go-round!
Where's the horse
For a kid that's black?

>   1942

Uncle Tom

Within—
The beaten pride.
Without—
The grinning face,
The low, obsequious,

这回转木马上

哪儿是黑人的位置?

先生,我想坐。

我打南方来

那里白人黑人

不能坐在一起。

在南方,火车上

有黑人车厢。

公共汽车黑人坐后面——

可是回转木马

分不出前后!

哪一个木马

能给黑孩子骑?

1942

汤姆叔叔[1]

里面——

是被揍扁的骄傲。

外面——

满脸甜蜜的笑,

低声下气,

---

[1] 美国女作家斯托夫人(1811—1896)所作《汤姆叔叔的小屋》中的主人公。现代美国黑人认为汤姆叔叔之逆来顺受是个可耻的形象。

Double blow,

The sky and servile grace

Of one the white folks

Long ago

Taught well

To know his

Place.

                                            1942

Silhouette

Southern gentle lady,

Do not swoon.

They've just hung a black man

In the dark of the moon.

They've hung a black man

To a roadside tree

In the dark of the moon

For the world to see

How Dixie protects

Its white womanhood.

鞠躬如仪,

逢迎驯顺,处处得体

这种人,多年前

白人

就教会他

懂得自己

什么身份。

1942

侧影

南方的女士们,
不必晕过去。
不过吊死个黑人
在无月的夜里。

他们把一个黑人
在无月的夜间
吊在村边树上
让全世界看见
南方是如何保护
白种妇女的贞节。

Southern gentle lady,
            Be good!
            Be good!

                                        1949

Harlem

What happens to a dream deferred?

Does it dry up
like a raisin in the sun?
Or fester like a sore—
And then run?
Does it stink like rotten meat?
Or crust and sugar over—
like a syrupy sweet?

Maybe it just sags
like a heavy load.

Or does it explode?

                                        1951

南方的女士们,
乖些!
乖些!

1949

哈莱姆

一个拖延的梦,会出什么事?

它会不会干枯
像太阳晒葡萄干?
或是像疮疖滚脓——
最后烂穿?
它会不会像臭肉腐烂?
还是像蜜糖上——
干出一层糖皮?

也可能它只是垂下
像负着千钧重压。

还是它会突然爆炸?

1951

Troubled Woman

She stands

In the quiet darkness,

This troubled woman,

Bowed by

Weariness and pain,

Like an

Autumn flower

In the frozen rain,

Like a

Wind-blown autumn flower

That never lifts its head

Again.

1959

Ardella

I would liken you

To a night without stars

Were it not for your eyes.

I would liken you

To a sleep without dreams

Were it not for your songs.

1959

痛苦的女人

她站在

幽静的黑暗里,

这痛苦的女人,

疲劳和忧伤

折磨着她,

好像一朵

秋天的花

淋在冻雨里,

好像一朵

秋风吹落的花

再也没能

把头抬起。

1959

阿黛拉

我要把你比成

一个无星的夜空,

若不是你的眼睛。

我要把你比成

一场无梦的睡眠,

若不是你的歌声。

1959

西奥多·罗斯克
(Theodore Roethke, 1908-1963)

罗斯克是20世纪四五十年代最著名的诗人之一。他的诗既有当时占优势的艾略特-兰色姆诗风那种严谨的技巧,又有舒卷自如的节奏;他个性强烈的诗风融合了传统技巧,某些杰出的篇章是两种诗风的结合。

他的祖父是德国移民,他的家族在密歇根州开一个花艺公司。罗斯克自幼在温室周围游玩,后来当他开始写诗,这些动植物成为他诗中生动的题材和象征。

他在大学读法律,有志做律师。但当他取得学位后,却彻悟他的一生事业应是写诗。经过长时间的摸索,33岁时,他出版了第一本诗集《开门的房屋》(1941年),受到热烈赞扬。20世纪40年代末,他的创作趋于成熟。到20世纪50年代,他连续获得诗歌三大奖:普利策奖(《觉醒》,1954年)、全国图书奖(《说给风听》,1959年)、波林根奖(《我认识一个女人》,1958年)。可惜的是,他有酗酒恶癖,1963年,于他创作力最鼎盛的时候突然离世。但留于人世不多的诗,已足以使他成为20世纪美国的重要诗人。

他的未结集作品在他去世后被收集于《远方的土地》一书中,1964年出版,次年被追赠全国图书奖。一直到20世纪60年代末,他的诗名一直在扩大。

罗斯克长期在大学里教授诗歌创作课程,他的学生中有好些后来成为有成就的诗人,因此罗斯克常被认为是当代美国诗的开拓者。

Open House

My secrets cry aloud.
I have no need for tongue.
My heart keeps open house,
My doors are widely swung.
An epic of the eyes
My love, with no disguise.

My truths are all foreknown,
This anguish self-revealed.
I'm naked to the bone,
With nakedness my shield.
Myself is what I wear:
I keep the spirit spare.

The anger will endure,
The deed will speak the truth
In language strict and pure.
I stop the lying mouth:
Rage warps my clearest cry
To witless agony.

1941

开门的房屋

我的秘密放声大呼。
我根本不需要舌头。
我心中有座开门的房屋,
我所有的门全部开足。
一首眼睛写的诗章
我的爱情,毫无伪装。

我的真情全部预知,
连这痛苦也自行揭开,
我剥光自己直到骨头,
裸露就是我的盾牌。
我自己就是我的衣服,
我让灵魂毫无用处。

愤怒能延续很长时间,
而行动将说明真相
用严格纯粹的语言。
我叫那嘴停止撒谎:
狂怒把我清晰的高呼
扭曲成轻率的痛苦。

1941

Root Cellar

Nothing would sleep in that cellar, dank as a ditch,
Bulbs broke out of boxes hunting for chinks in the dark,
Shoots dangled and drooped,
Lolling obscenely from mildewed crates,
Hung down long yellow evil necks, like tropical snakes.
And what a congress of stinks!—
Roots ripe as old bait,
Pulpy stems, rank, silo-rich,
Leaf-mold, manure, lime, piled against slippery planks.
Nothing would give up life:
Even the dirt kept breathing a small breath.

1948

Cuttings

Sticks-in-a-drowse droop over sugary loam,
Their intricate stem-fur dries;
But still the delicate slips keep coaxing up water;
The small cells bulge;

储球根的地窖

地窖里湿得像阴沟,一切都醒着,
球根破匣而出,在黑暗中寻找缝隙,
新芽钻出发霉的篓子,
低悬着,下流地晃荡,
垂着长长的凶恶的黄头颈,像热带的蛇。
好一个臭味的大杂烩!——
根熟透了,像陈年的钓饵,
多浆的茎,像饲料仓一样腥臭刺鼻,
腐叶,肥料,石灰,堆在滑溜的板上。
谁也不放弃生命:
甚至尘土也在呼出轻微的气息。

1948

插枝

插在瞌睡中,低垂在糖一般的土上,
它们错综的纤毛干枯了;
但纤巧的枝条还在诱水上升,
微小的细胞在膨胀;

One nub of growth

Nudges a sand-crumb loose,

Pokes through a musty sheath

Its pale tendrilous horn.

                                        1948

Cuttings (Later)

This urge, wrestle, resurrection of dry sticks,

Cut stems struggling to put down feet,

What saint strained so much,

Rose on such lopped limbs to a new life?

I can hear, underground, that sucking and sobbing,

In my veins, in my bones I feel it,—

The small waters seeping upward,

The tight grains parting at last.

When sprouts break out,

Slippery as fish,

I quail, lean to beginnings, sheath-wet.

                                        1948

一个生长的节点
把砂屑推松,
苍白的卷须似的触角
穿透了朽烂的芽鞘。

1948

续插枝

干燥的枝条冲动、挣扎、复活,
剪断的茎搏斗着把脚放到地上,
何等的圣人,如此奋力,
用被砍断的四肢攀进新的生命?

我能听见,在地下,那吮吸和啜泣,
我血管里,骨头里,也感觉到,——
小小的水珠往上升,
紧绷的土粒终于分开。
当嫩芽突然进出,
像鱼一样滑溜,
我害怕,倚向开端,刚出鞘全身湿透。

1948

Night Crow

When I saw that clumsy crow

Flap from a wasted tree,

A shape in the mind rose up:

Over the gulfs of dream

Flew a tremendous bird

Further and further away

Into a moonless black,

Deep in the brain, far back.

1948

The Far Field (Excerpts)

IV

The lost self changes,

Turning toward the sea,

A sea-shape turning around,—

An old man with his feet before the fire,

In robes of green, in garments of adieu.

A man faced with his own immensity

Wakes all the waves, all their loose wandering fire.

The murmur of the absolute, the why

夜半乌鸦

当我见到笨拙的乌鸦

从枯树上扑翅惊起,

我心中升起一个影子:

越过梦境的海湾

一个巨鸟展开长翼

越飞越远,遥远地

飞进没有月光的暗夜,

飞进脑海中深远的过去。

1948

远方的土地(选段)

四

迷失的自我变化着,

转身向大海,

像海一般转身,——

一个老人在炉边烘脚,

穿着绿袍,告别的服饰。

一个人面对他自己的广袤,

吵醒海浪,和海浪上漫游的火。

绝对的低语,生命的秘密,

Of being born falls on his naked ears.

His spirit moves like monumental wind

That gentles on a sunny blue plateau.

He is the end of things, the final man.

All finite things reveal infinitude:

The mountain with its singular bright shade

Like the blue shine on freshly frozen snow,

The after-light upon ice-burdened pines;

Odor of basswood on a mountain-slope,

A scent beloved of bees;

Silence of water above a sunken tree:

The pure serene of memory in one man,—

A ripple widening from a single stone

Winding around the waters of the world.

1964

落到他裸露的耳朵上。
他的梦魂像狂风疾驰
静息在阳光照耀的蓝色高原。
他是万物的终结,是最后的人。

一切确定的事物都有不确定性:
山的阴影那么明亮,
就像新雪上蓝光幽幽,
像冰封的松树映着夕阳;
山坡上椴树的气息,
与蜜蜂那种可爱的香味;
淹没的树上,水那么宁静:
像孤独者的记忆那么清纯,——
漪涟从一块石头开始
扩展到全世界的海面。

1964

兰达尔·贾雷尔
(Randall Jarrell, 1914-1965)

在第二次世界大战的炮火中,美国产生了一些"战争诗人",贾雷尔可以说是这些诗人的代表,有论者甚至认为他"实际上是唯一的能写出第二次世界大战的诗人"。

贾雷尔在南方田纳西读中学,后在美国新批评派的发源地范德比尔特大学就学,师从新批评领袖人物约翰·克罗·兰色姆,毕业后又在兰色姆主持的凯尼恩学院执教,应当说他是新批评的私淑弟子之一。1942年他参军,并且在战场上写出他最出名的一些战争诗篇。或许我们会觉得奇怪,这些诗中根本就没有对反法西斯战争的正义性和对美国军人勇敢作战的赞扬,只能读到战争的恐怖,杀人者与牺牲者一样的盲目,而人在这庞大的战争机器中渺小而可怜。这些对战争经验的描绘使贾雷尔离开了新批评派的"非个性化"诗路,虽然其诗形式的严谨和结构之细密仍看得出他所受艾略特-兰色姆传统的影响。

战后贾雷尔执教于大学,并写了六本诗集和三本文学批评文集。在这些批评中,他对此时已上升到文坛统治地位的新批评派大加攻击。他后期的诗始终没能摆脱战争年代的痛苦经验,似乎回忆始终没有完全褪尽,他的诗对人生的痛苦和理想幻灭的失望似乎特别敏感,所以罗伯特·罗厄尔称他为"这一代最令人心碎的英语诗人"。

贾雷尔1965年在穿过一条公路隧道时被车撞死,很多人认为他是自杀,这相当令人惋惜——他的诗歌创作根基深厚,本应取得更多的成绩。

Eighth Air Force

If, in an odd angle of the hutment,
A puppy laps the water from a can
Of flowers, and the drunk sergeant shaving
Whistles *O Paradiso!*—shall I say that man
Is not as men have said: a wolf to man?

The other murderers troop in yawning;
Three of them play Pitch, one sleeps, and one
Lies counting missions, lies there sweating
Till even his heart beats: One; One; One.
O murderers! ... Still, this is how it's done:

This is a war... But since these play, before they die,
Like puppies with their puppy; since, a man,
I did as these have done, but did not die—
I will content the people as I can
And give up these to them: Behold the man!

I have suffered, in a dream, because of him,
Many things; for this last saviour, man,
I have lied as I lie now. But what is lying?
Men wash their hands, in blood, as best they can:
I find no fault in this just man.

                                    1945

第八航空队

在临时兵营的一个冷僻角落

罐头瓶里插着花,而小狗在舐

罐头里的水,喝醉的军曹刮脸

吹着《哦,天堂!》》[1]——难道我能否认

人对人是豺狼这句常言?

别的杀人者鱼贯而入,呵欠连天;

三个人掷钱游戏,一个睡觉,

一个计算飞行次数,躺着流汗,

直到他的心也跳着数:一、一、一。

《哦,杀人者!》……但事情就是这么做的:

这是战争……既然他们在死之前,

还像小狗跟小狗一样玩;既然作为人

我跟他们一样行事,却能身免——

我尽我所能让大家高兴,

让他们各自取乐:瞧这人!

为了他我在梦中吃多少苦,

为了人,这最后的救世主,

我过去撒谎,现在撒谎。但什么是谎?

人用血洗手,尽量洗清楚:

这正直的人,我看不出有何错处。

1945

---
[1] 当时流行的一出歌剧中的咏叹调。

The Death of the Ball Turret Gunner[1]

From my mother's sleep I fell into the State,

And I hunched in its belly till my wet fur froze.

Six miles from earth, loosed from its dream of life,

I woke to black flak and the nightmare fighters.

When I died they washed me out of the turret with a hose.

1945

The Range in the Desert

Where the lizard ran to its little prey

And a man on a horse rode by in a day

They set their hangars: a continent

Taught its conscripts its unloved intent

In the scrawled fire, the singing lead—

Protocols of the quick and dead.

The wounded gunner, his missions done,

Fired absently in the the range's sun;

---

[1] A ball turret was a plexiglass sphere set into the belly of a B-17 or B-24, and inhabited by two .50 caliber machine guns and one man, a short small man. When this gunner tracked with his machine guns a fighter attacking his bomber from below, he revolved with the turret; hunched upside down in his little sphere, he looked like the foetus in the womb. The fighters which attacked him were armed with cannon firing explosive shells. The hose was a steam hose.

旋转炮塔射手之死 [1]

我从母亲的沉睡中落到这个状态,
在肚子里佝偻着,直到湿绒毛冻结,
离地六英里,从生命之梦中解脱,
我醒来,看见黑色的高射炮,这梦魇似的战斗机。
我死后,他们用水龙把我从炮塔冲走。

1945

沙漠靶场

蜥蜴扑向小小的猎物
有一天骑者飞驰而过
他们建好机库:一个大陆
教新兵理解它那不可爱的意图
在这乱窜的火中,歌唱的铅弹——
是活者和死者拟定的草案。
受伤的炮手,他的使命已了结,
还在茫然地向靶场的太阳射击;

---

1 贾雷尔自注:"旋转炮塔"是装在 B-17 或 B-42 轰炸机腹部的有机玻璃球体,装备着两架 0.5 英寸口径的机枪,可容一个身材矮小的人。当枪手向由低处袭来的战斗机射击时,他与炮塔同时旋转,他在这小球中弓着背倒转时,很像子宫中的胎儿。攻击轰炸机的战斗机装备着发射爆破弹的炮。水龙是一种蒸汽管。

And, chained with cartridges, the clerk
Sat sweating at his war-time work.
The cold flights bombed—again, again—
The craters of the lunar plain....

All this was priceless: men were paid
For these rehearsals of the raids
That used up cities at a rate
That left the coals without a State
To call another's; till the worse
Ceded at last, without remorse,
Their conquests to their conquerors.
The equations were without two powers.

Profits and death grow marginal:
Only the mourning and the mourned recall
The wars we lose, the wars we win;
And the world is—what it has been.

The lizard's tongue licks angrily
The shattered membranes of the fly.

1948

那职员挂着墨盒好像锁链,
浑身流汗坐着做战时工作。
一次又一次——冷酷的机群,
炸出月球平原上的巨坑……

这一切是无价的:人拿了钱
就是为了演习空袭投弹,
空袭消耗城市,真是神速,
只留下炭块,没有一个国家
还想要别人的炭;直到一边最终,
落败,毫无悔恨地让出
他们征服的地方给征服者。
方程式中不可能有两个大国。

利润和死亡一齐变得微不足道:
只有哀悼者和被哀悼者会去想
我们输掉的战争,我们赢得的战争;
世界依旧——一如往昔时辰。

蜥蜴的舌头愤怒地舔着
苍蝇那已经破碎的翅膜。

1948

Well Water

What a girl called "the dailiness of life"
(Adding an errand to your errand. Saying,
"Since you're up..." Making you a means to
A means to a means to) is well water
Pumped from an old well at the bottom of the world.
The pump you pump the water from is rusty
And hard to move and absurd, a squirrel-wheel
A sick squirrel turns slowly, through the sunny
Inexorable hours. And yet sometimes
The wheel turns of its own weight, the rusty
Pump pumps over your sweating face the clear
Water, cold, so cold! you cup your hands
And gulp from them the dailiness of life.

1965

井水

姑娘们称为"日常生活"的东西
（差使你又差使你，说是：
"你既然已经起来……"把你当作
工具的工具的工具）就是从古井里
打世界的底层抽出的井水。
你汲水的唧筒已经生锈，
很难摇动，太荒唐，像松鼠轮子
一只病鼠在慢慢推动，度过充满
阳光的冷酷的时光。但有时
轮子突然会自己转动，生锈的
唧筒也抽出清水，喷到你
流汗的脸上，清凉，多清凉！你以手
一掬，从中猛饮一口日常生活。

1965

西尔维娅·普拉斯
(Sylvia Plath, 1932-1963)

20世纪50年代末开始的自白诗运动中,不仅有罗伯特·罗厄尔和约翰·贝里曼这样的诗坛老将,而且也卷入了不少青年诗人,其中女诗人普拉斯的成就特别耀眼。虽然她在30来岁时自杀,但她几本薄薄的诗集至今仍得到人们的赞赏。普拉斯的诗醉心于在自我与客观世间的关系中发掘混乱,几乎把自白诗那种悲剧式的自我揭露推到了极端,她的某些诗使人感到如在梦魇中喊叫,在她眼中,自我和世界靠痛苦而结合。

普拉斯的父亲是归化美国的德国人,她在英国剑桥大学毕业后,嫁给英国颇负盛名的诗人泰德·休斯,他们定居在英国,生了一女一子。1960年她出版了第一本诗集《巨大的雕像》,反响不大。休斯在20世纪60年代初另有新欢,使普拉斯十分痛苦。1962年冬天,普拉斯单独带两个孩子寓居伦敦。1963年2月11日,她吸煤气自杀。据她的传记作家写道,她以前已经有过几次未遂的自杀尝试。

她的遗稿陆续编成《爱丽尔》(1965年)、《渡湖》(1971年)和《冬树》(1971年)出版,在美国诗坛上激起了热烈的反应,成为自白诗运动的又一个高潮。近几十年来,普拉斯在诗歌史上的地位似乎越来越高。但也有人有不同意见,例如自白派的领袖罗伯特·罗厄尔就说她把自己的痛苦写得"太过分"。

但普拉斯也有诗写生活的快乐,也有诗讽刺西方的社会现实,她的早逝使美国诗坛损失了一位大有前途的女诗人。

Man in Black

Where the three magenta
Breakwaters take the shove
And suck of the grey sea

To the left, and the wave
Unfists against the dun
Barb-wired headland of

The Deer Island prison
With its trim piggeries,
Hen huts and cattle green

To the right, and March ice
Glazes the rock pools yet,
Snuff-colored sand cliffs rise

Over a great stone spit
Bared by each falling tide,
And you, across those white

Stones, strode out in your dead
Black coat, black shoes, and your
Black hair till there you stood,

穿黑衣的人

在那儿,三条洋红的
防波堤把灰色大海的
推挤和吮吸接过来

搁到左边,波浪
松开拳头,面对着
鹿岛监狱那暗褐色的

铁丝网围起的海岬,
右边有整齐的猪圈
鸡舍和牲畜饲草,

而三月的冰使山岩中的
水潭平滑如镜,
鼻烟色的砂石岩礁

俯临着布满石头的漫长沙嘴,
每次退潮被水清扫一遍,
而你,从这些白色的石头

之间,迈步走出,穿着
无光泽的黑大衣,黑鞋,
黑头发,最后你站定

    Fixed vortex on the far
    Tip, riveting stones, air,
    All of it, together.

                    1960

Medallion

By the gate with star and moon
Worked into the peeled orange wood
The bronze snake lay in the sun

Inert as a shoelace; dead
But pliable still, his jaw
Unhinged and his grin crooked,

Tongue a rose-colored arrow.
Over my hand I hung him.
His little vermilion eye

Ignited with a glassed flame
As I turned him in the light;
When I split a rock one time

像远处岛尖上那不动的
漩涡,把石头,天空,
把一切铆固在一起。

　　　　　　　　1960

徽章

大门雕着星星和月亮
木色像剥皮的橘子,旁边
青铜的蛇躺在阳光中

不动弹,像条鞋带;死了
但仍旧柔软,他的下巴
散了关节,带着古怪的笑,

而舌头,像玫瑰色的箭。
我把他挂在手上。
当我在阳光中翻动他

他那朱红色的小眼睛
燃着玻璃似的火苗;
有一次我敲碎一块石头

The garnet bits burned like that.
Dust dulled his back to ocher
The way sun ruins a trout.

Yet his belly kept its fire
Going under the chainmail,
The old jewels smoldering there

In each opaque belly-scale:
Sunset looked at through milk glass.
And I saw white maggots coil

Thin as pins in the dark bruise
Where innards bulged as if
He were digesting a mouse.

Knifelike, he was chaste enough,
Pure death's-metal. The yard-man's
Flung brick perfected his laugh.

                                        1960

里面的晶粒也是这样燃烧。
灰尘把他的背弄成暗褐色
就好像阳光毁灭一条鳟鱼。

但他的腹部仍有火焰
在锁子甲下依旧炽燃,
在每片不透明的腹鳞之中

古老的钻石在隐隐烧着:
透过毛玻璃看到的日落。
我看到在发黑的伤处

白色的蛆蜷曲,像针一样细,
那部位内脏肿胀,似乎是
他在消化一只老鼠。

真像一把刀子,他够贞静的,
纯粹的死神的武器。看院人
扔的砖头使他的笑容完美。

1960

Morning Song

Love set you going like a fat gold watch.
The midwife slapped your footsoles, and your bald cry
Took its place among the elements.

Our voices echo, magnifying your arrival. New statue.
In a drafty museum, your nakedness
Shadows our safety. We stand round blankly as walls.

I'm no more your mother
Than the cloud that distills a mirror to reflect its own slow
Effacement at the wind's hand.

All night your moth-breath
Flickers among the flat pink roses. I wake to listen:
A far sea moves in my ear.

One cry, and I stumble from bed, cow-heavy and floral
In my Victorian nightgown.
Your mouth opens clean as a cat's. The window square

晨歌

爱发动你,像个胖乎乎的金表。
助产士拍拍你的脚掌,你单调的叫喊
在世界万物中占定一席之地。

我们的声音呼应,放大了你的到来。新的雕像。
在多风的博物馆里,你的赤裸
使我们的安全蒙上阴影。我们围站着,墙一般空白。

云渗下一面镜子,映出它自己
在风的手中慢慢消失的形象,
我同云一样,不是你的母亲。

整夜,你飞蛾般的呼吸
在平放的粉玫瑰间闪动。我醒来静听:
我耳中有个远方的大海。

一声哭,我从床上滚下,母牛般笨重,
穿着满是花纹的维多利亚式睡衣。
你嘴张开,干净得像猫的嘴。方形的窗

Whitens and swallows its dull stars. And now you try

Your handful of notes;

The clear vowels rise like balloons.

1965

The Applicant

First, are you our sort of a person?

Do you wear

A glass eye, false teeth or a crutch,

A brace or a hook,

Rubber breasts or a rubber crotch,

Stitches to show something's missing? No, no? Then

How can we give you a thing?

Stop crying.

Open your hand.

Empty? Empty. Here is a hand

To fill it and willing

To bring teacups and roll away headaches

And do whatever you tell it.

Will you marry it?

It is guaranteed

变白,吞没了暗淡的星。而你现在
试唱你满手的音符;
清脆的元音像气球般升起。

         1965

申请人

首先,你是我们同类吗?
你戴不戴
玻璃眼珠?假牙?拐杖?
背带?钩扣?
橡皮乳房?橡皮胯部?

针线缝合,有东西缺失?没有?没有?那么
我们能否设法给你一件?
别哭,
伸开手。
空的?空的。这是只手

正好补上,它愿意
端来茶杯,揉走头痛
你要它干什么它都干。
你愿意娶它吗?
它保证能

To thumb shut your eyes at the end
And dissolve of sorrow.
We make new stock from the salt.
I notice you are stark naked.
How about this suit—

Black and stiff, but not a bad fit.
Will you marry it?
It is waterproof, shatterproof, proof
Against fire and bombs through the roof.
Believe me, they'll bury you in it.

Now your head, excuse me, is empty.
I have the ticket for that.
Come here, sweetie, out of the closet.
Well, what do you think of *that*?
Naked as paper to start

But in twenty-five years she'll be silver,
In fifty, gold.
A living doll, everywhere you look.
It can sew, it can cook,
It can talk, talk, talk.

在你临终时为你翻下眼睑,
溶解忧愁。
我们用盐制成新产品。
我注意到你赤身裸体,
你看这套衣服如何——

黑色,有点硬,但挺合身,
你愿意娶它吗?
不透水,打不碎,
防火,防穿透房顶的炸弹,
你放心,保证你入土时也穿这衣服。

现在看看你的头,请原谅,空的。
我有张票子可供你选用。
来啊,小乖乖,从柜子里出来,
怎么样,你看如何?
开始时像一张纸般一无所有,

二十五年变成银的,
五十年,变成金的。[1]
一个活的玩偶,随你怎么端详。
会缝纫,会烹调,
还会说话,说话,说话。

---

1 西方俗称,结婚一周年为纸婚,25周年称银婚,50周年称金婚。

It works, there is nothing wrong with it.
You have a hole, it's a poultice.
You have an eye, it's an image.
My boy, it's your last resort.
Will you marry it, marry it, marry it.

1965

Poppies in October

Even the sun-clouds this morning cannot manage such skirts.
Nor the woman in the ambulance
Whose red heart blooms through her coat so astoundingly—

A gift, a love gift
Utterly unasked for
By a sky

Palely and flamily
Igniting its carbon monoxides, by eyes
Dulled to a halt under bowlers.

很派用场，不出差错。

你有个伤口，它就是敷药。

你有个眼睛，它就是图像。

小伙子，这可是最后一招。

你可愿意娶它，娶它，娶它。

1965

十月的罂粟花

今晨的云霞也做不出这么漂亮的裙子，
救护车里的女人也没有
她红色的心穿过大褂，骇人地开花——

一件礼物，爱情的礼物
完全是不请自来，
来自

苍白地，火苗闪闪地
点着了一氧化碳的天空，来自
礼帽下呆滞的眼睛。

O my God, what am I

That these late mouths should cry open

In a forest of frost, in a dawn of cornflowers.

1965

Words

Axes

After whose stroke the wood rings,

And the echoes!

Echoes traveling

Off from the center like horses.

The sap

Wells like tears, like the

Water striving

To re-establish its mirror

Over the rock

That drops and turns,

A white skull,

Eaten by weedy greens.

Years later I

Encounter them on the road—

哦上帝,我是什么人

能使这些迟来的嘴张口大喊,

在凝霜的森林,在矢车菊的清晨?

1965

词儿

斧子

每劈一下,树木就玎玲鸣响,

听这回声!

回声传得很远

像骏马,从中心驰开。

树汁

眼泪般涌出,好像

水努力

在岩石上

重新架镜。

它滴下,旋转,

一个白色的颅骨,

被野草的浓绿啃光。

多少年之后,我

在路上又遇到他们——

Words dry and riderless,

The indefatigable hoof-taps.

While

From the bottom of the pool, fixed stars

Govern a life.

1965

Daddy

You do not do, you do not do

Any more, black shoe

In which I have lived like a foot

For thirty years, poor and white,

Barely daring to breathe or Achoo.

Daddy, I have had to kill you.

You died before I had time—

Marble-heavy, a bag full of God,

Ghastly statue with one gray toe

词儿干了,失去骑者,

但有永不疲倦的马蹄声。

这时候

许多恒星,从池底上

控制一个生命。

1965

爹爹[1]

你再不能这么做,再也不,

你是黑色的鞋子

我像只脚,关在里面

苍白、可怜,受三十年苦,

不敢打嚏,气不敢出。

爹爹,我早该杀了你。

我还没动手你就死去——

大理石般沉重,一袋子神灵,

鬼一般的雕像,一个脚趾灰色,

---

[1] 普拉斯的父亲是波兰籍德国人,15岁就随家移居美国,在波士顿教德语,攻昆虫学。普拉斯两岁时其父去世。关于此诗,普拉斯表示:"这首诗出自一个有恋父情结的女孩之口。她父亲死时她认为父亲是神,事实是她父亲是个纳粹分子,而母亲很可能有犹太血统,因此情况就复杂了。在女儿身上这两种压力结合而互不相让——她不得不再次将那可怕的小寓言表演一遍,才能摆脱它。"

Big as a Frisco seal

And a head in the freakish Atlantic
Where it pours bean green over blue
In the waters off beautiful Nauset.
I used to pray to recover you.
Ach, du.

In the German tongue, in the Polish town
Scraped flat by the roller
Of wars, wars, wars.
But the name of the town is common.
My Polack friend

Says there are a dozen or two.
So I never could tell where you
Put your foot, your root,
I never could talk to you.
The tongue stuck in my jaw.

It stuck in a barb wire snare.
Ich, ich, ich, ich,

像旧金山的海豹一样大

像奇异的大西洋上一个头颅
在那里海水把豆绿倒入天蓝
在美丽瑙塞特海滩外的海水里。
从前我经常祈求你复生。
Ach，du。[1]

说德国话，住波兰城
那个被战争，战争，战争
的压路机碾平的小城。
但这地名太普通。[2]
我的波兰籍朋友

说有一两打之多。
所以我从来不清楚
你住在哪里，到过何处。
我从来没能跟你说话。
舌头在嘴里卡住。

在装铁刺的陷阱里卡住。
Ich，ich，ich，ich，[3]

---

1 德语：啊，你。
2 普拉斯的父亲出生于波兰格拉布夫。
3 德语：我，我，我，我。

I could hardly speak.
I thought every German was you.
And the language obscene

An engine, an engine
Chuffing me off like a Jew.
A Jew to Dachau, Auschwitz, Belsen.
I began to talk like a Jew.
I think I may well be a Jew.

The snows of the Tyrol, the clear beer of Vienna
Are not very pure or true.
With my gipsy ancestress and my weird luck
And my Taroc pack and my Taroc pack
I may be a bit of a Jew.

I have always been scared of *you*,
With your Luftwaffe, your gobbledygoo.
And your neat mustache
And your Aryan eye, bright blue.
Panzer-man, panzer-man, O You—

我从来说不出。

我觉得每个德国人都是你。

这语言太下流

像一架引擎,一架引擎

把我当犹太人一般发落。

该去达豪、奥斯威辛、贝尔森[1]的犹太人。

我开始像犹太人一般谈吐。

我满可以成为犹太人。

蒂罗尔[2]的雪,维也纳的白啤酒

都不纯粹也不真实。

我的吉卜赛先祖,我的奇特命运,

我的塔罗牌[3],我的塔罗牌,

我有几分像犹太人。

我始终害怕你,

你有空军,你有官腔,

你修剪整齐的胡子

你的雅利安眼睛,透亮的蓝,

装甲兵,装甲兵,哦你——

---

1 都是纳粹集中营。
2 奥地利西南部一州。
3 中世纪流行的一种算命用的纸牌。

Not God but a swastika
So black no sky could squeak through.
Every woman adores a Fascist,
The boot in the face, the brute
Brute heart of a brute like you.

You stand at the blackboard, daddy,
In the picture I have of you,
A cleft in your chin instead of your foot
But no less a devil for that, no not
Any less the black man who

Bit my pretty red heart in two.
I was ten when they buried you.
At twenty I tried to die
And get back, back, back to you.
I thought even the bones would do.

But they pulled me out of the sack,
And they stuck me together with glue.
And then I knew what to do.
I made a model of you,

不是上帝,而是一个卐字,
如此漆黑,天空也无法穿过。
每个女人都崇拜法西斯分子,
脸上挂着长靴,野蛮的
野蛮的心,长在野兽身上,像你——

你站在黑板旁边,爹爹,
我有你的一张照片,
一条裂痕长在下巴上,而不是脚上[1]
但你依然是魔鬼,不比
那穿黑衣的人[2]差半分,那人

把我可爱的红心一咬两半。
我十岁时他们埋葬了你。
二十岁时我有死的意图
回到,回到,回到你的身边,
哪怕你已成白骨。

但他们把我从袋里拖出,
用胶水把我粘住。
此后我才知道该如何做,
我给你做了一个雕塑,

---

[1] 西方民间传说魔鬼的脚是裂趾的。
[2] 这里普拉斯指她的丈夫休斯。

A man in black with a Meinkampf look

And a love of the rack and the screw.
And I said I do, I do.
So daddy, I'm finally through.
The black telephone's off at the root,
The voices just can't worm through.

If I've killed one man, I've killed two—
The vampire who said he was you
And drank my blood for a year,
Seven years, if you want to know.
Daddy, you can lie back now.

There's a stake in your fat black heart
And the villagers never liked you.
They are dancing and stamping on you.
They always *knew* it was you.
Daddy, daddy, you bastard, I'm through.

1965

一个黑衣人,脸像《我的奋斗》[1]

一个老虎凳和拇指夹的爱好者。
我说我招供,我招供。
因此,爹爹,我终于结束。
黑色的电话线连根剪断,
声音无法爬行通过。

要是我杀一个人,就等于杀两个人——
那吸血鬼,他说他就是你
他吸我的血已有一年,
说明确些,已有七年。
爹爹,你现在可以安息。

你肥胖的黑心算盘打得太足
村民们从来就不喜欢你。
他们踩在你身上跳舞,
脚底是你,他们完全清楚。
爹爹,爹爹,你这混蛋,我结束。

1965

---

[1] 希特勒的自传,封面是希特勒的头像。

The Couriers

The word of a snail on the plate of a leaf?
It is not mine. Do not accept it.

Acetic acid in a sealed tin?
Do not accept it. It is not genuine.

A ring of gold with the sun in it?
Lies. Lies and a grief.

Frost on a leaf, the immaculate
Cauldron, talking and crackling

All to itself on top of each
Of nine black Alps.

A disturbance in mirrors,
The sea shattering its grey one—

Love, love, my season.

1965

快邮

蜗牛的词在树叶的盘里?
那不是我的,别收下。

密封铁皮罐里的醋酸?
别收下。那不是真的。

一个金指环,里面有个太阳?
谎言。谎言加上痛苦。

叶子上的霜,洁净的
大锅,说着话,噼啪地响

在阿尔卑斯山九座黑色的
峰顶上与自己对谈。

镜中的一场动乱,
大海击碎了它的灰色——

爱情,爱情,我的季节。

1965

Crossing the Water

Black lake, black boat, two black, cut-paper people.

Where do the black trees go that drink here?

Their shadows must cover Canada.

A little light is filtering from the water flowers.

Their leaves do not wish us to hurry:

They are round and flat and full of dark advice.

Cold worlds shake from the oar.

The spirit of blackness is in us, it is in the fishes.

A snag is lifting a valedictory, pale hand;

Stars open among the lilies.

Are you not blinded by such expressionless sirens?

This is the silence of astounded souls.

                                                    1971

渡湖

黑湖,黑船,两个黑纸剪出的人。
在这里饮水的黑树往哪里去?
它们的黑影想必一直伸到加拿大。

荷花丛中漏过来一星点光线。
莲叶不让我们匆忙穿过:
扁平的圆叶,老在做阴暗的劝告。

从桨上摇下一片片冰冷的世界。
我们怀着黑色的精神,鱼也如此。
一个断树桩举起苍白的手告别;

星星在浮莲之间开放,
塞壬[1]如此面无表情,没把你变成石头?
这是惊呆的灵魂特有的寂静。

1971

---

[1] 希腊神话中半人半鸟的海妖,常以歌声使航船覆没。

渡湖

黑湖,黑船,两个黑纸剪出的人。
在这里饮水的黑树往哪里去?
它们的黑影想必一直伸到加拿大。

荷花丛中漏过来一星点光线。
莲叶不让我们匆忙穿过:
扁平的圆叶,老在做阴暗的劝告。

从桨上摇下一片片冰冷的世界。
我们怀着黑色的精神,鱼也如此。
一个断树桩举起苍白的手告别;

星星在浮莲之间开放,
塞壬[1]如此面无表情,没把你变成石头?
这是惊呆的灵魂特有的寂静。

1971

---

[1] 希腊神话中半人半鸟的海妖,常以歌声使航船覆没。